soul fitness

*Secrets to Cracking
the Immortality Code*

SHIREEN CHADA

Soul Fitness
Secrets to Cracking the Immortality Code

© Copyright 2023 — Shireen Chada

Published by Release Your Wings (www.releaseyourwings.net),
a Brahma Kumaris/USA (www.brahmakumaris.org/us) production.

All rights reserved. This book is protected by the copyright laws of the United States of America. This book may not be copied or reprinted for commercial gain or profit. The use of short quotations or occasional page copying for personal or group study is permitted and encouraged. Permission will be granted upon request.

Quotes without attribution are original to the author.

Paperback: 978-1-941883-08-2 ISBN 13

Ebook: 978-1-941883-09-9 ISBN 13

For worldwide distribution.

Cover design by Michael Mackintosh

My heartfelt thanks to Baba for inviting me to craft this book. Throughout the endeavor, a tune played in my mind: "I'm merely an instrument." To You, I dedicate this work that You enabled. You are always with me.

Also by the Author

Books

True Hollywood Blockbuster – The Making of Divine Heroes
Oh My Goodness! – Grow Your Virtues and Flourish

Meditation Albums

The 8 Spiritual Powers
Real Reflections
The Sweet Melody of Silence

TABLE OF CONTENTS

1 Welcome to Spiritual Wholeness and Immortality 1
How Is This Different from Other Books?.. 2
My Journey from Emptiness to Spiritual Awakening 2
Signs of Soul Illness.. 10
Quiz: Assessing Your Soul's Health... 11
What Is Soul Fitness?... 14
Maximizing the Benefits of This Book.. 15

2 Cracking the Immortality Code 19
Embracing Immortality Through Soul Fitness................................. 21

3 Soul Fitness Regimen 23
Soul Fitness Exercise 23
Soul Fitness Meditation 24
Why Open-Eyed Meditation?... 25
Understanding the Structure of the Book.. 26
A Well-Rounded Soul Fitness Regimen to Follow............................ 28
Soul Fitness to Help Alleviate Stress, Anxiety, and Depression 29

4 Material vs. Spiritual: Unveiling the Soul Within......... 31
Eternal Wholeness: A Meditation on the Real You......................... 33

5 Embracing the Truth That Will Set You Free 35
Embracing Your Inner Spiritual Trainer: You Are
Love Meditation.. 37
Understanding Spiritual Truths Across Time and Space 39
Embracing the Truth That Will Set You Free Meditation............... 40

6 Worldview Matters: How Perspectives Shape and Drive Our Lives 43
Shine a Light on Your Worldview and Embrace the Sublime 45
Adopt the Inside-Out Worldview and Revitalize Yourself 46
Embracing the Inside-Out Worldview for Spiritual Growth Meditation 47

7 The Importance of Assumptions in Spirituality 49
Your Intrinsic Nature Is Love Meditation 51

8 The Power of Acceptance in Spiritual Transformation .. 53
Difference Between Blind Faith and Acceptance 56

9 Discovering Who I Am as Consciousness 57
Visualizing the Soul as Light 58
Exploring the Location of the Soul 59
Immortality of the Soul 60
The Power of Self-Realization Meditation 61

10 Discovering the Fountain of Youth Through Soul Fitness 63
Meditation on Releasing Limiting Labels and Embracing Your True Potential 65
Hypnotized by Labels: Breaking Free from Body Identity 66
Steps To Discovering the Fountain of Youth 68
The Fountain of Youth Within: Journeying to Your Radiant Soul Identity Meditation 69

11 The Journey Within: Unleashing the Hero in You Through Thoughts 71
Stage 1: Initiation Into Thoughts 72
Stage 2 – Slay the Dragon of Negative Thoughts 73
Stage 3 – Know the Familiar Foe of Useless Thoughts 73
Stage 4 – Transcend the Status Quo of Mundane Thoughts 73
Stage 5 – Be Guided by Your Friend (Positive Thoughts) 74
Stage 6 – Find the Ultimate Treasure: Pure, Eternal Thoughts for Soul Fitness 74
Awakening the Spiritual Fitness Hero Meditation 76

12 Soul Fitness Warm-Ups: Easing Into Your Spiritual Journey ... 79
Enhanced Shavaasana: A Journey to Self-Awareness ... 80
Soul Fitness Breathing: A Holistic Approach to Reducing Stress ... 82
Healing Your Body With Light ... 83
The Power of Thought Observation ... 84
Free Your Mind: Escaping the Shackles of Negativity ... 85
Embodying an Attitude of Gratitude ... 87
Healing Thoughts, Healing Self ... 88
Refresh Your Mind, Revive Your Spirit ... 90
Creating Your Serenity Prayer ... 91

13 Easy Soul Fitness: Stages on the Journey ... 93
Understanding: The First Stage on the Inner Journey ... 94
Reflection: The Second Stage on the Inner Journey ... 95
Concentration: The Third Stage on the Inner Journey ... 96
Experience: The Fourth Stage on the Inner Journey ... 97

14 Uncovering the Primary Qualities of the Soul ... 99
Love: A Journey Toward Wholeness ... 100
Peace: Embracing Soulful Serenity ... 102
Purity: Restoring the Soul's Innocence ... 103
Bliss: A Joy Beyond the Senses ... 104
Knowledge: The Endless Quest for Truth ... 105
Meditation: Rediscovering Intrinsic Qualities ... 107

15 Mastering Your Mind ... 109

16 Sculpting Mental Muscles: Unlocking the Mind's Potential ... 111
Chiseling Away Stress: Carving Inner Peace ... 112
Cradling the Inner Child: Nurturing Your Mind With Love ... 114
Dismantling the Seven Deadly Cs: Loving the Mind ... 115
Soul Foodie: Feeding Your Mind With Care ... 117
Soul Reprieve: Embracing Moments of Rest ... 118
Echoes of Compassion: Radiating Love to the World ... 120

17 Awakening the Inner Buddha: Cultivating Your Discernment 123
Harnessing the Power of the Intellect for Mental Clarity............. 124

18 Strength Training the Soul: Exercising the Intellect ... 127
Learning to Trust Yourself to Make the Right Choices................. 128
Taking Courageous Steps: Cultivating Willpower...................... 129
Journey to Conviction... 131
Breaking the Illusion: Unmasking Fear............................. 132
Embracing Reality: The Art of Letting Go.......................... 134
Illuminating and Purifying the "I"................................ 136
The Power of Concentration in Finding Silence..................... 137

19 Spiritual Muscle Memory: Awakening the Soul's Original Qualities 139
Building Spiritual Equity: Awakening the Blissful You Through Focus Meditation...................................... 142

20 Consciousness Triad: Exploring the Mind, Intellect, and Sanskars 143
Understanding the Mind, Intellect, and Sanskars Loop for Deep Transformation... 144
A Simple Test to Awaken Pure Sanskars.............................. 147
Engaging the Triad: From Decision to Conviction Exercise........... 147

21 Healing the Spiritual Heart: Embracing Love, Compassion, and Connection 149
Deep Self-Love: Healing the Spiritual Heart for Resilience......... 150
Achieving Inner Harmony: The Connection Between Heart, Mind, and Intellect.. 151
Cultivating a Joyful Heart for Emotional Well-Being................ 152

22 Soul Cardio: Six Transformative Exercises to Strengthen Your Spiritual Heart 153
Kickstart Your Day With Pure, Loving Feelings...................... 154
Cultivating Self-Love.. 155
Elevating Your Perspective: Overcome Disappointment and Empower Yourself.. 156

Finding Joy in Your Own Company *158*
Soothing the Soul, Healing Your Heart *160*
The Art of Balanced Living: Mastering Love and Detachment *162*

23 Memory Track: The Bridge Between Conscious and Subconscious Realms 165
Clearing the Soul's Memory Track *166*
Memory Track Alchemy: Transforming Negativity Into Stillness .. *168*

24 Unlocking Inner Bliss: The Benefits of Awakening Your Conscience 171
Conscience: The Soul's Compass *172*
Lessons From Dadi Janki's Unwavering Spirit *173*
Awakening Your Conscience Meditation *175*

25 Soul Fitness on the Go: Reaping the Rewards 177
Cultivating a Balanced Relationship With the Body *179*
The Thinker: Discovering the Thinking, Feeling Soul *180*
The Role of the Soul in Driving the Body *181*
Awakening the Memory of Immortality *182*
Path to Freedom Through the Question: Who Am I? *183*
Viewing the Body as a Costume for the Immortal Actor Within ... *184*
Experiencing Being an Eternal Voyager *185*
Embracing the Innate Imperishable Qualities of the Soul *186*
Mastering the Soul, the Life Force of the Body *186*
The Sacred Temple: Revering the Body *187*
Beyond Gender: Embracing Soul Awareness for Spiritual Transformation *188*
Soul and Body: A Partnership of Electricity and Light Bulb *189*
The Puppeteer Within *190*
The Guest Within *191*
From Seed to Sprout: Awakening Hidden Potential *192*
Opening the Third Eye *193*
Timer Meditation: A Technique for Enhancing Focus *194*

26 Command Your Senses, Master Yourself 197
Overcoming Illusion and Gaining Control Over Our Eyes 198
Tuning The Ears: Overcoming Emotional Turmoil 200
Practicing Detachment from Sense of Smell 201
Overcome Emotional Eating to Cultivate Balance 202
Mastering the Sense of Touch 203
Mastering the Art of Speech 204

27 Stress Buster Meditations 205
Dealing With Depression 205
Dealing With Insomnia 208
Build Better Relationships 213
Combat the Stress of Consumerism 214
Deal With Work Stress 217

28 Choosing Soul Fitness 219

Acknowledgments 222

1

WELCOME TO SPIRITUAL WHOLENESS AND IMMORTALITY

Soul Fitness: Secrets to Cracking the Immortality Code is a transformative book that guides you toward inner peace, clarity, and profound joy. With its practical techniques and insightful lessons, this book will help you:

- Experience Deep Joy: Achieve pure consciousness and profound joy through the Soul Fitness practices and wisdom.

- Address Stress and Anxiety: Identify and manage the root causes of stress and anxiety for improved emotional well-being.

- Cultivate a Focused Mind: Improve mental focus and clarity by applying the provided techniques.

- Uncover Innate Spiritual Powers: Discover hidden abilities such as enhanced intuition, increased empathy, and greater creativity.

- Discover a Sense of Purpose: Connect with your true self through Soul Fitness and uncover a more profound sense of purpose and meaning in life.

How Is This Different from Other Books?

Many spiritual books overlook the importance of acquiring the wisdom of spiritual reality, which transcends the present illusion. Recognizing this gap, I present crucial knowledge in this book to enable the soul to embrace self-realization, true freedom, and immortality naturally.

Another aspect frequently missing from spiritual literature is a how-to guide to unveil the soul's potential and ultimate perfection. In this book, I present meditation after meditation, exercise after exercise to help access one's divine resources, such as peace, love, truth, innocence, and joy. By incorporating the elements present in this book, individuals can embark on a more comprehensive and transformative journey toward enlightenment and immortality.

My Journey from Emptiness to Spiritual Awakening

I Had What I Wanted, but I Wasn't Happy
Nearly thirty years ago, after landing my first job in America, I couldn't help but wonder, "Now what?" This job was realizing a dream that had begun during my childhood in South India in the 1970s. Raised in a culture that expected most women to marry, raise families, and adhere to extended family traditions, I craved the freedom that came with financial independence. So, I chased my professional aspirations with gusto.

This pursuit led me to the US, where I earned a graduate degree in Engineering and secured my first job. Despite achieving my lifelong goal, I was far from happy. In fact, I was utterly disappointed, and a deep sense of emptiness haunted me. I was also troubled by an intense, visceral sensation of the profound sorrow in the world.

During this time of restlessness, I found myself browsing through a rental car location, waiting to rent a vehicle. As if by fate, my gaze fell upon a brochure that seemed to call out to me. Its opening line pierced me, asking, "Are you experiencing the sorrow of the world?" Spellbound by the serendipity, I decided to visit the meditation center it advertised. There, I discovered a fascinating new world of spirituality, offering me a sense of comfort and hope. It opened the door to a whole new dimension of life I'd never known.

A New World
As an engineer with a foundation in logic and reason, I found myself intrigued by the mysterious world of spirituality, seeking to comprehend the relationship between science and mysticism - and what existed beyond the material realm. I was introduced to a range of spiritual disciplines and practices designed to awaken a deeper part of myself. At first, some of these practices were challenging, but I did them anyway, knowing deep in my soul that they would allow me to pass through into a higher state and enter a richer enlightened state of being.

As I delved deeper into the realm of spirituality, my meditation practices began to bear fruit. Early on, I had an incredible experience of God's love pouring into the soul, a deep feeling of belonging to God, and feeling God's power filled me. I experienced profound feelings of love, belonging, awe, and wonder all at the same time, creating an extraordinary emotional landscape within me.

The more I practiced these methods, I encountered moments of immense joy and boundless gratitude as if I had won a grand jackpot. The feeling was as if this path was predestined and something I had yearned for across many lifetimes.

Mystical Experiences at 4:00 AM

One of the surprising things I learned was that there was a "magic hour" for meditation between 4:00 am and 5:00 am when the atmosphere was more conducive to deeper practice. When my teacher first told me about this, I thought she was joking. How could I possibly wake up at 4:00 am? I was used to going to bed at around 2:00 am so the whole idea seemed ridiculous. But despite my initial resistance, I committed to waking up at 4:00 am every day and seeing for myself what happened. This was an incredibly challenging task but I tried it anyway. To make sure I woke up, I used three alarm clocks strategically placed throughout my tiny apartment. One was tucked away in the closet, another one in the kitchen, and the last one in the bathroom. By the time I deactivated the first two alarms and reached the last one, I was resolute in starting my meditation with a refreshing shower.

One morning, at around 4:20 am, I had an extraordinary out-of-body experience, journeying into a world of infinite divine light and constant peace. I felt completely and totally liberated flying up into the home of souls, up into the presence of God. As I found myself separated from my physical body, serenity and stillness enveloped me. My mind was free from thoughts, focused only on the essence of being. Simultaneously, I experienced a profound connection to God and a deep contentment with everything unfolding around me. After that experience, I felt everyone belonged to me, and I belonged to everyone. This filled me with feelings of compassion and unity.

Following this awakening, I deeply contemplated the direction of my life, pondering my purpose and the course I should take. How could I give back? What could I do to serve?

Thus began a 30-year adventure into higher awareness and service with over 20,000 hours of meditation experience. During this time (which I will share briefly) I developed powerful practices that work even under extreme situations so you can benefit easily even if you're just starting out.

A New Adventure Begins
With an aspiration to make a difference, I embraced the position of coordinator at the meditation center. During this time, I tried to balance the demands of a full-time job, managing the center, dealing with all the students, and navigating the pressures of daily life. As my responsibilities, workload, and stress kept increasing, all I wanted was a spiritual life but instead, I seemed to be running around all the time, being pulled this way and that.

There were days when exhaustion from work, financial concerns, and ensuring the smooth operation of the center weighed heavily on me. As I sat for meditation, my restless mind would wander incessantly. I found myself questioning how to tame this unruly "monkey mind." To navigate this challenge, I sought to devise strategies that would allow me to experience stillness even in these trying circumstances. Many of the practices outlined in this book address questions such as: How can we maintain a higher state of being while under great pressure? What are the practical spiritual methods that really work?

At one point, my body became seriously ill, requiring a substantial dose of steroids to keep it alive. The medications plunged me into an unexpected emotional abyss. It was during this period that I developed some of the practices you'll discover in this book. Through sheer determination and the strength of these life-saving practices, I tenaciously clawed my way out of the dark pit with the force of 20 nails.

This was when a transformative moment occurred. I had a profound realization that I will have to live with myself for eternity. Since I am never going to get away from myself, I need to truly appreciate myself and relish the experience of being alive.

This understanding led to a significant paradigm shift, prompting me to attune even deeper to the inner workings of the soul and master them rather than seek an escape. I came to terms with the fact that no external force would change my life; the responsibility for cultivating a joyful, triumphant, and meaningful life rested solely upon me. And I needed to find all the methods to live a fully successful, happy, peaceful, and wonderful life. There is nowhere to hide so why not master the art of living? Why not fully embrace Soul Fitness?

As my own cheerleader and coach, I embraced this truth, uncovering peace within myself and rising from the shadows of despair with some of these meditation exercises you'll discover in this book.

As the months and years passed, all kinds of people came to learn meditation at the center. And I was able to see firsthand how these methods changed their lives for the better. But from time to time, small and large challenges arose to test me and see if these techniques really worked under all conditions.

One evening, I returned to the center when I was confronted by a former mafia member who had been attending classes. When I arrived, I found him there entertaining a lady friend. I informed him the center was not meant for such purposes and requested the key back. Enraged, he stood up with an evil look in his eyes and threatened to shoot me, painting the wall with the whites of my brain. At that moment, despite my initial desire to roll him off the planet, I felt free from fear and at peace. He stormed off and never returned. In the quiet moments after this, I feel that all the practices I'd done had protected me and I was never alone.

Life moved on with all its twists and turns, and the more I kept up with these Soul Fitness practices, the more liberated I felt. For a while, I thought I was finally free from challenges, but life had yet another test for me.

Can Soul Fitness Help Survive a Life-Threatening Illness?
Despite eating well and living a healthy life, I was shocked to be diagnosed with breast cancer one day. Initially, I was consumed by self-pity. As I underwent a mastectomy and subsequent treatments, I learned to nurture my body with love and care, incorporating walking and yoga into my routine. I began to merge spiritual and physical maintenance, practicing spiritual exercises during my workouts. These "spiritual drills" trained my mind to be fit, and I discovered that I could pursue both spiritual and physical well-being simultaneously without sacrificing one for the other. This is the other element of Soul Fitness - how we can use our mind, heart, and attitude toward life to heal ourselves inter-

nally and externally. Many people have cancer and are unable to cope emotionally. I believe these Soul Fitness practices once again saved my life. And more than that, they helped me refine the methods that I could share with others.

It was after surviving cancer that I truly grasped the transformative potential of spirituality and the healing it could bring to both my life and the lives of those around me. Embracing an authentic spiritual path could be challenging at times, much like exercise, but if we persevere, it could lead to profound joy, clarity, and inner peace.

Why I Wrote This Book?
This book you hold in your hands is a culmination of my deep 30-year journey and aims to enrich your life with the insights I've gained through experiences.

I now have accumulated nearly three decades of meditation experience. As a result, I have developed a holistic approach to soul wellness that I've been sharing with thousands of people at the center and in our work online.

I've seen people go from depressed to happy and free, from addicted to various substances to clean, sober, and liberated. I've seen souls racked with fear become peaceful and able to embrace their lives fully. These practices really work, and they work even under the most difficult conditions.

While this approach, just like physical exercise, may be demanding at first, it ultimately leads to increased strength, well-being, and happiness.

As a prolific creator of meditations, an author, retreat leader, workshop facilitator, and presenter on the Release Your Wings YouTube channel, I've had the great pleasure of seeing how these innovative and empowering techniques have impacted numerous lives. And it's my honor to connect with you too.

I invite you to join me on this transformative journey to freedom, happiness, peace, wellness, and inner power.

May you allow the wisdom in this book to guide you toward a more fulfilling life. Now is your chance to embark on your journey to Soul Fitness and experience firsthand the profound transformation that unfolds, positively transforming the landscape of your life forever.

These methods will give you the strength, courage, and capacity to experience your highest self and experience a life far beyond anything you knew possible. By delving into this book, you'll gain insight into nurturing the soul, and throughout this illuminating voyage, you'll discover the significance of Soul Fitness in achieving immortal life.

Are you ready to experience Soul Fitness?

Signs of Soul Illness

Drawing from my extensive background in spiritual exploration and teachings, I have come to understand that self-awareness is the key to unlocking the soul's potential. As we navigate this journey together, let's first see the signs of both physical and spiritual well-being.

Physical Illness Signs	Physical Fitness Signs
High Blood Pressure	Energized
Diabetes	Strong
Fatigue	Good Immune System
High Cholesterol	Healthy Heart
Insomnia	Good Mental Health

Soul Illness Signs	Soul Fitness Signs
Stress	Happy
Anxiety	Relaxed
Depression	Loving
Worry	Peaceful
Restlessness	Enthusiastic

The next step to becoming soul fit is recognizing the signs of a soul in need. To help you identify your condition, we've created a short quiz that will give you a better understanding of where you currently stand.

Quiz: Assessing Your Soul's Health

As you prepare to take the quiz, bear in mind that in today's world, we find ourselves surrounded by an abundance of unhealthy food options and lifestyle habits that can lead us down a path of illness and misguided choices. Likewise, our hearts and souls are often exposed to a myriad of negative influences, such as harmful information, misleading news, and shallow values.

Please remember, this is not a reflection of who you are. It's all too easy to get swept away in a current of negativity, but it's important to gently remind ourselves to put in the effort to rise above it. Regardless of the outcome of the following quiz, you're already on the right track simply by reflecting on these topics.

1. **How often do you feel stress and anxiety?**
   a. Rarely
   b. Sometimes
   c. Often
   d. Always

2. **Do you feel a flood of worry when you experience a new ache, pain, or ailment in the body?**
   a. Rarely
   b. Sometimes
   c. Often
   d. Always

3. **Do you have a sense of purpose or meaning in your life?**
   a. Yes, I have a clear sense of purpose
   b. I have a vague idea, but I'm not completely sure
   c. I'm still searching for my purpose
   d. I don't believe I have a purpose

4. **How would you rate your ability to let go?**
   a. I have an almost zen-like ability to let go of anything that is no longer serving me.
   b. Letting go comes naturally to me and I don't have much difficulty moving on from things.
   c. I am generally able to let go of things, but it can take me some time to process and move on.
   d. I find it very difficult to let go of things, even when it's necessary.

5. **How much do you value and respect yourself?**
   a. I have a high level of self-respect and respect for others
   b. I value and respect myself, but struggle to prioritize my own needs at times
   c. I have low self-respect and struggle to prioritize my own needs
   d. I have no self-respect and do not prioritize my own needs at all

6. **How often do you practice forgiveness, both towards yourself and others?**
   a. Frequently
   b. Sometimes
   c. Rarely
   d. Never

7. **How often do you engage in negative self-talk or criticize yourself?**
   a. Rarely or never - I am kind and compassionate to myself
   b. Occasionally - I am aware of negative self-talk but it still happens
   c. Often - negative self-talk is a frequent pattern for me
   d. Always - I am very harsh and critical towards myself

8. **How often do you meditate and focus on your inner peace?**
   a. Almost every day
   b. A few times a week
   c. Occasionally
   d. Rarely or never

9. **When things don't go your way, how do you usually react?**
   a. I never feel disappointed or discouraged
   b. I rarely feel disappointed or discouraged
   c. I feel disappointed and discouraged occasionally
   d. I feel disappointed and discouraged often

10. **How often do you dwell on negative events or outcomes?**
    a. I never dwell on negative events or outcomes
    b. I rarely dwell on negative events or outcomes
    c. I sometimes dwell on negative events or outcomes
    d. I often dwell on negative events or outcomes

    Scoring: For each question, assign the following points: a=1, b=2, c=3, d=4. Add up your total score. Interpreting Your Score:

- 5-10: You may not require this book, but it will help reinforce and expand your existing knowledge.

- 11-15: Consider implementing the strategies provided in this book to improve the soul's well-being.
- 16-20: The soul could use some healing. This book will provide you with valuable guidance to help you restore balance and harmony to your inner self.
- 21-25: The soul is showing clear signs of illness. It's important to address these issues immediately, and this book can serve as an essential resource on your journey to wholeness

When reflecting on your quiz results, kindly treat yourself with understanding and empathy. If you or someone else is dealing with an illness, remember that providing kindness and compassion is much more meaningful than attributing fault or guilt.

What Is Soul Fitness?

You are a spiritual being having a human experience through your body. You are the thinking, feeling being within; the body is just a dress, a covering. The soul is the real you. Soul Fitness means when the real you, the soul, is healthy. To be a healthy soul means for the soul to understand its true identity, its real purpose, and what happiness is.

Soul Fitness is a spiritual approach to achieving a healthy and fulfilled life. It is about getting your soul into shape; just as physical fitness is about getting your body into shape. The whole principle of Soul Fitness is that just as there is a naturally healthy state of the body, there is an original, healthy state of the soul. You are unhappy if your body is not well, so imagine how you will feel if your soul is not in shape. Just as the right food and exercise make the body healthy. Similarly, we can bring our consciousness to a healthy state by feeding our mind a diet of "nutritious" thoughts and doing spiritual "exercises."

Spiritual exercises mean training our minds to do certain psychological thought practices. These exercises are like mental workouts that help break self-sabotaging thought patterns and activate our original, pure selves. By regularly feeding our minds "nutritious" thoughts, we can naturally experience peace, love, and joy. Our thoughts perpetuate both mental and behavioral cycles in our life, and Soul Fitness is a way to break free from negative cycles and achieve a healthy soul.

Recognizing what does not constitute Soul Fitness is equally important, as doing so helps us break free from detrimental habits.

- Indulging in physical pleasures without acknowledging our true essence can ultimately cast shadows over our lives.
- Focusing solely on the disparities between physical forms rather than recognizing the spiritual equality shared by all living beings leads us astray into ignorance.

Maximizing the Benefits of This Book

This book is designed to help you develop a healthier and more balanced life by nurturing the soul. We have outlined five essential steps to get the most out of this experience. These steps will guide you in setting clear intentions, treating yourself with love and kindness, practicing patience and persistence, gradually building your spiritual strength, and focusing on continuous improvement. Embrace these principles and embark on a fulfilling path toward a better you.

Set your intention: Take some time now and ask yourself, "What do I want to gain from this book?" Setting a personal intention for your well-being and growth is important.

Approach the process with love and kindness for yourself. Treat yourself with compassion as you embark on this journey of self-empowerment.

Be patient and persistent. Fitness doesn't happen overnight. Those who achieve it do so by consistently incorporating small exercises into their daily routine. Over time, these small actions accumulate, resulting in a fitter and healthier person as new habits are formed.

Build your spiritual muscles gradually. This program is designed to help you strengthen your spiritual muscles slowly but surely. Be patient with yourself and trust the process.

Don't dwell on your current struggles or suffering. Instead, focus on taking the next step toward improvement. Remember that every small step counts and contributes to your overall progress.

By following these guidelines, you can make the most of this book and its teachings, ultimately leading to a healthier and more fulfilled soul.

**Access free meditations to go deeper
into your quest for immortality:**

These Soul Fitness meditations will pave the way for your true spiritual nature to unfold, illuminate, and spread joy to yourself and the world.

Go here to get access now:

shireenchada.com/soulfitness

2

CRACKING THE IMMORTALITY CODE

This book takes on the central question of how one can achieve immortality. The primary obstacle to unlocking the secret to immortality is our fixation on the mortal body. The modern world is obsessed with extracting every ounce of enjoyment from a body that inevitably deteriorates and dies. It's akin to an individual becoming so accustomed to, and comfortable with, illness or disability that they find the notion of wellness disconcerting. Unraveling the immortality code stems from an unwillingness to confront who we are as spiritual beings.

The attempts of scientists to alleviate human suffering and enhance the quality of life are praiseworthy. Yet, their approach can be compared to the ancient Greek myth of Icarus.

Icarus and his father Daedalus, tried to escape from the labyrinth of King Minos with wings made of feathers and wax. Daedalus warned Icarus not to fly too close to the sun, as the heat would melt the wax holding the feathers together. However, Icarus, intoxicated by the thrill of flying, ignored his father's wise counsel and soared too high. His wings melted, and he plummeted into the sea, meeting his tragic end.

This tale reveals the perils of arrogance and overconfidence, which can cloud judgment and obscure valuable guidance. Despite their noble intentions, some scientists refuse to consider wisdom from ancient texts about the true nature of our being. They insist that the physical body encompasses our entire existence. As the poignant tale of Icarus demonstrates, humility and open-mindedness are crucial in our quest to crack the immortality code.

Science acknowledges significant barriers in the pursuit of physical immortality. Currently, there is no material key to eternal life, and it is increasingly improbable that science will unlock this mystery within our lifetimes or ever. However, the code can be deciphered if one is simply willing to confront the truth.

The conundrum arises from the tantalizing potential for immortality, seemingly within our grasp. Yet we must embrace our true immortal selves to unlock the mystery. Our reluctance to wholeheartedly acknowledge and embrace our immortal spiritual essence presents our biggest challenge, much like a spiritual variant of dissociative identity disorder, in which an individual has difficulty recognizing their higher self.

The quest for immortality is, fundamentally, a journey of self-realization. As we delve deeper into understanding our true nature as spiritual beings, we uncover the inherent wisdom within us. By cultivating self-awareness, we can transcend the limitations of our physical existence and embrace our natural immortality.

Embracing Immortality Through Soul Fitness

Put simply: nurturing the soul unlocks the secret to immortality. Soul Fitness means to make the soul healthy and fit. If we feel wonderful when our body is fit, imagine your joy when the real you, the soul, is healthy and strong. Getting you there is the purpose of this book.

In this book, you'll learn how to prioritize inner health for a fabulous life experience. By exploring the contents of this book, you will learn to care for the soul and thus build emotional and spiritual strength. During this enlightening journey, you will clearly see that Soul Fitness is key to embracing immortality.

3

SOUL FITNESS REGIMEN

This book is a culmination of thirty years of dedication, exploration, and personal transformation. Over the past three decades, I have delved deep into the realms of the spirit, refined my understanding, and developed techniques to help us become spiritually aware. This journey has led me to formulate a Soul Fitness Regimen or a comprehensive step-by-step guide to a spiritual awakening that consists of a set of Soul Fitness exercises and meditations that can empower you to uncover your true identity.

Soul Fitness Exercise

A Soul Fitness exercise is a series of mental steps performed in a specific order, designed as a cognitive workout. Each step requires an appropriate mental posture, ultimately fortifying the soul. Remember and execute these steps in sequence. By consistently practicing these exercises, you'll enhance your ability to focus and train your mind to do your own meditations.

SOUL FITNESS MEDITATION

Soul Fitness meditations are soothing, contemplative passages that typically conclude a chapter, allowing the mind to assimilate its key points. As you read, simply ponder the content without exerting mental strain. Allow yourself to engage with the material in a relaxed and thoughtful manner. Through these reflective meditations, you can achieve a more profound grasp of the content and nurture a sense of tranquility.

I have at times also referred to Soul Fitness exercises and meditations as practices within this book.

Soul Fitness exercises and meditations differ from each other but at times they interlace each other to form meditations or complement each other to contribute to a comprehensive approach to Soul Fitness. Upon completing ample exercises from the book, you will be well-equipped to develop your personalized meditations. A point in case here is, I used various exercises to help cultivate the stress-buster meditations in chapter 27.

This book will primarily focus on the Brahma Kumaris (BK) meditation approach. This distinctive form of meditation encourages contemplation on eternal principles to foster spiritual empowerment. With its open-eyed method, the BK meditation is adaptable, uncomplicated, and seamlessly integrates into everyday life.

Why Open-Eyed Meditation?

I encourage you to do all the meditations with your eyes open. We recommend this because:

- Practicing open-eye meditation helps you integrate it with daily life. It makes it easier to go between meditation and regular tasks seamlessly and enables you to deepen your practice.
- Keeping your eyes open during meditation can help you stay awake.
- Meditation with your eyes open enhances focus and awareness.
- Open-eye meditation encourages you to maintain a soft focus on a specific point, which can help minimize visual distractions.

If you discover that meditating with your eyes open is too challenging, try meditating with your eyes slightly closed and gaze downward. Remember, you can learn and adapt to anything, so it's ideal to experiment with both methods until you can successfully meditate with your eyes open.

Understanding the Structure of the Book

The book is designed for you to first uncover valuable insights and then follow the practices. This progression will make your journey to Soul Fitness smoother and more rewarding.

In summary, the book consists of:

Chapters 4, 5, and 6 delve into why we need Soul Fitness. How it can help us connect with something larger than ourselves, and find purpose and meaning.

Chapters 9, 10, 11, 14, 15, 17, 19, 20, 21, 23, and 24 explore the concept of the soul as the spiritual essence that represents the core of a person, transcending the physical body. They also uncover thoughts, the mind, the intellect, the impressions, the heart, the memory track, the conscience, and the subconscious aspects of the spirit. These chapters provide a framework for understanding the principles and mechanisms of the soul. A solid understanding of how the soul works and what is happening in our inner lives enables us to make informed decisions when applying the practices and evaluating the possible consequences of Soul Fitness exercises.

Chapters 12, 16, 18, 22, 25, and 26 consist of fifty practices. These exercises have evolved with me over the decades on my spiritual journey. I have painstakingly practiced, tested, and refined them over time. I have consolidated them within these six chapters so you can reference them if you choose to design your personalized Soul Fitness regimen. They are designed for:

Skill Development: The exercises provide a structured approach to implementation and improvement, helping you to master Soul Fitness.

Precision and Accuracy: The techniques outlined in this book will help you improve precision and accuracy in your Soul Fitness journey.

Consistency: These Soul Fitness techniques will help you achieve positive outcomes consistently.

The exercises are created to lift your consciousness, much like lifting weights in a gym, and can be classified as follows:

- Soul Fitness Warm-Ups: Easing into Your Spiritual Journey (Chapter 12)
- Sculpting Mental Muscles: Unlocking the Mind's Potential (Chapter 16)
- Strength Training the Soul: Exercising the Intellect (Chapter 18)
- Soul Cardio: Exercises to Strengthen Your Spiritual Heart (Chapter 22)
- Soul Fitness on the Go: Reaping the Rewards (Chapter 25)
- Command Your Senses, Master Yourself (Chapter 26)

A Well-Rounded Soul Fitness Regimen to Follow

The recommendation is to do a minimum of 30 minutes in the morning and 30 minutes in the evening/night.

AM Schedule (30 Minutes):
Begin with a Soul Fitness Warm-up from Chapter 12. You can choose any warm-up exercise to ease into your spiritual journey.

Followed by three days a week of Sculpting Mental Muscles from Chapter 16.

Three days a week Strength Training the Soul from Chapter 18.

One day a week from Chapter 26 -- Command Your Senses, Master Yourself.

PM Schedule (30 Minutes):
Three days a week of Soul Cardio from Chapter 22.

Four days a week of Stress Busters from Chapter 27.

Throughout the Day:
This is very important: During the day, pause every hour and do one Soul Fitness on the Go exercise from Chapter 25.

Imagine a man named Mike, who constantly consumes unhealthy food, is overweight, and lacks physical fitness. If Mike approaches a gym trainer and requests to lose 100 pounds and achieve optimal shape by the next day, it would sound absurd, wouldn't it?

Similarly, we often hold unrealistic expectations when it comes to spiritual practices. After performing a single meditation session or, in our context, one Soul Fitness exercise, we may wonder why our hearts haven't healed or why we haven't attained peace.

So have patience, dear readers. Consistency is the key. This is a results-oriented fitness program. As we delve into the pages, we will uncover exceptional strategies to nurture the soul's energy and resilience on our journey to total Soul Fitness. We can establish a harmonious equilibrium and secure lasting spiritual well-being by integrating these potent practices into our daily routines.

To reiterate, the soul possesses an innate state of well-being – this is Soul Fitness. Our original spiritual nature is fit and strong, but ignorance conceals it. Ignorance, lust, ego, greed, and anger are like the unwanted fat layers in the body. These layers are the soul's enemies. Following a good Soul Fitness regimen can help us discard unwanted layers and make the soul fit and strong.

Soul Fitness to Help Alleviate Stress, Anxiety, and Depression

The Soul Fitness exercises featured in chapters 12, 16, 18, 22, 25, and 26 provide a comprehensive strategy for managing stress, depression, and anxiety. Through consistent practice, you will gradually experience a shift away from these symptomatic emotions. It is essential to recognize that stress, anxiety, and depression are symptoms rather than diseases. Addressing them as diseases may result in overlooking the root cause. This book and its contents aim to address the underlying sources of our symptomatic emotions and feelings to foster overall emotional well-being.

4

MATERIAL VS. SPIRITUAL: UNVEILING THE SOUL WITHIN

The core concept of Soul Fitness lies in the belief that akin to a natural healthy state for the body, there exists an innate, wholesome state for the soul. Just as an unwell body affects happiness, an out-of-shape soul impacts well-being. By nourishing our minds with metaphysical concepts, we can achieve a balanced, healthy state of consciousness.

And, to comprehend spiritual principles, it's essential to distinguish between matter and spirit. Matter represents the physical, tangible world, while spirit refers to the intangible, transcendent aspects of existence. Recognizing these fundamental differences enables a deeper understanding of who we are as spirits. Let's explore this duality to cultivate Soul Fitness.

In essence, there are two types of things in the world - spiritual entities that are eternal and temporary objects that never fully exist. Let's take a house as an example. In reality, it is just matter, or material energy like in physics, shaped into the form of a house. Bricks, mortar, wood, glass, and other material things are brought together and given a name because of their specific arrangement.

But ultimately, it is just a collection of matter that will eventually cease to exist in that particular shape. All the different elements will return to their original state of matter.

The body is similar to a house. Like the house, the body can be broken down into its component parts, like arms, legs, and different organs. We can call the body Shireen or Bill or John or Mary. But ultimately, it is just material energy with a particular shape and a given name. We all know that at some point we will cease to exist as a body. So, this life form is not our real existence. It is just a bunch of matter with a temporary shape.

On the contrary, our soul or spirit will always be in existence. It is not that we put love, peace, thoughts, and consciousness together and call it a soul. No, the soul always exists. That is what you really are, an eternal soul, and you can never really be anything else. Your body must perish – it has a life span. You, the soul, never perish. You are eternally your real self, the soul. This is the fundamental distinction between matter and spirit. They are simply two different kinds of energy.

For example, now my persona as a soul-in-a-body is Shireen Chada, who navigates this world as a female Indian American. I'm an eternal soul beyond my present persona. This is why even though the body changes constantly (cell regeneration), there is still a continuous person – me. To grasp spiritual reality, we need to understand these two fundamentally different kinds of things – matter and spirit.

Four important things to remember about the spirit or soul:

1. It is whole – it is never put together, nor can it be broken down.
2. It always exists.

3. This spiritual being, the spirit, is the life force of the body.
4. The soul is the thinking, and feeling being in the body.

When we continually feed our minds a "nutritious" diet of eternal concepts, we will be on our way to Soul Fitness.

Eternal Wholeness:
A Meditation on the Real You

* *Find a comfortable position, sit quietly, and take a few deep breaths.*

* *Firstly, remember that your spirit is whole. It is never put together nor can it be broken down. It is a beautiful and perfect essence – this is who you really are. You, the soul, are waiting to be seen by you. Take a moment now and just acknowledge that you are a wholly spiritual being.*

* *Secondly, you, the spirit, always exist. You are timeless and transcend the physical world. Allow yourself to feel your eternal nature, and know that you will continue to exist beyond the limits of time and space.*

* *Thirdly, you, the spirit, are the life force of your body. Take a moment now and feel the life force flowing through your body, and recognize this is who I am.*

* *Lastly, you, the soul, are the thinking, feeling being in your body. You, the spirit, experience the world. Take a moment to reflect on your thoughts and feelings – these are coming from you, the spirit.*

* *Slowly and gently come out of this meditation taking these four important things with you into your day.*

5

EMBRACING THE TRUTH THAT WILL SET YOU FREE

I was born in India, in our small ancestral village, at home. When my mother was due to deliver me, she couldn't get to a hospital because a curfew was imposed in the area due to some precarious political conditions. We had a lot of relatives living in close proximity to us in our village. So, a bunch of my aunts were my mother's midwives. I had this very public birth (I've had many complaints to my mom for doing this) and every time one of my aunts saw me, they used to tell me, "I saw you being born. You used to look so cute. What happened to you?". Gee! Thanks!! Right?

Cell regeneration is the natural process of replacing cells, tissues, and even entire organs. According to researchers at Stanford University, the body replaces itself with a new set of cells every seven to ten years.

A few years back, I met some of my aunts who were my welcome party to this world. I hadn't seen some of them in over twenty years. But they instantly recognized me. How come they knew me even though not a single visible cell in my body was the same as on the day I was born or when they last saw me?

There is something constant in me. Despite the old cells dying and new cells forming in my body, there is something that is always there, which is my essence, my spirit. My spirit is the one that helps people recognize me even if they are meeting me after decades. I am that spirit, that soul, the animating life force of my body that is constant through all the physical changes. My aunts recognized this soul, this eternal being within my body.

Therefore, we should shift our consciousness into thinking that, "I am a soul and I have this body." It's not the other way around where we falsely believe that "I am a body that has a soul." When we deeply explore this subtle yet crucial distinction between soul and body, we can truly experience freedom. And this freedom is the essence of a healthy, nutritious diet for the fitness of our soul, or our spirit.

We can improve our spiritual fitness by deepening our understanding of the soul through the exploration of spiritual truth. The Oxford Dictionary defines truth as, "That which is true or in accordance with fact or reality." Although many things are true, here we are concerned with a particular category of true things – those relating to our soul, or our spiritual selves.

We follow a good nutrition plan and engage personal trainers who study how the body works to tell us which muscles and how often to exercise and what we should eat for our long-term physical health. It's great that some people can advise us to help maintain our physical health because if we don't take care of our bodies, we set ourselves up for serious trouble.

Fortunately for us, we can learn to be our own spiritual personal trainers. Many of us are going through extreme stress, anxiety, depression, and trauma because we haven't grasped how the soul functions. We can help ourselves out of such predicaments if we understand how our soul functions. To understand how the soul functions we need to understand the spiritual truth.

Let's begin our spiritual personal training process by first learning about spiritual truth, which is an eternal concept.

When we know that something always exists, then we know that that concept is a spiritual truth. For example, love. Love doesn't have a life span and true love doesn't have any restriction of time on it. So, we can go a step further and say, "I, the soul, am love. I will always experience love. I will always give love. I am eternally love.". Or we can also assume that love is an original, eternal quality of the soul. Let's meditate on this.

Embracing Your Inner Spiritual Trainer: You Are Love Meditation

* *Begin by finding a comfortable place to sit. Take a few deep inhalations and exhalations.*

* *As you breathe, remind yourself that you are a spiritual being on a journey to discover eternal truths. Focus on the concept of love, an enduring and limitless force that exists within you.*

* *Now, silently repeat: "I, the soul, am love." Feel the warmth and power of this statement in your heart. Allow yourself to fully embrace this truth, recognizing that love is an inherent quality of you, the soul.*

* *Now, see yourself as an eternal being, radiating love and compassion. Visualize this love as a vibrant energy ema-*

nating from your core and extending outwards into the world around you.

* *Repeat: "I will always experience love. I will always give love. I am eternally loved." Feel the strength and certainty of these words, allowing them to become your personal mantra.*

* *Allow yourself to be enveloped in the warmth of your love, feeling the stress, anxiety, depression, and trauma gently dissolve as you embrace your true nature. Know that you are a powerful force for good in the world, capable of cultivating love and healing for yourself and others.*

* *As you continue to breathe, take a moment to bask in the serenity and peace that comes with recognizing your eternal love. Gently bring your awareness back to your surroundings.*

* *Carry the knowledge of your eternal love with you, knowing that you can access this powerful energy at any time by embracing your role as your own spiritual personal trainer.*

Understanding Spiritual Truths Across Time and Space

Eternal is a really long time. It is hard for some of us to grasp eternity so let's take a smaller number, say a million years. I existed a million years ago, I exist today, and I will exist a million years from now. Now, let's extrapolate and consider what constitutes spiritual or in other words, eternal truth. For any concept or thing to be an eternal truth, it has to fit the following criteria:

Is constant, and does not change over time. That is, it is the same today, was 5000 years ago, and will be a million years from now.

Is universal, the same for all people on the planet and it applies to everyone equally.

Is impartial, the same from all perspectives -- it is the same no matter who views it.

Reveals our divine nature when we reflect on it, and we experience a state of divinity and bliss beyond our senses.

At the core of all religious scriptures and teachings, there is a certain spiritual or eternal truth, eternal framework, or a timeless concept. Our job as rational beings is to find and reflect on that core. Because reflecting on the core truth will set us free.

Every single human being on this planet wants freedom. When someone doesn't follow the laws of the land, what is the first thing that is taken away from them? Their freedom, then they are put in prison. But here we are talking about spiritual freedom. Not just the physical freedom to do whatever we want or when we want, but to really be free from dependencies, fears, limiting beliefs, and insecurities. The spirit experiences the freedom, the joy of being untethered and unbound when we reflect on the core timeless concepts.

The eternal framework we are talking about here is not tactile. You can't touch it, you can't taste it, you can't physically measure it, nor can you see it. It is a spiritual entity that can be grasped with awareness and understanding. For this, we have to accept that there is something more to us than our physical body.

Then the question arises, how can we infuse ourselves with this eternal truth? We have to pursue it with a single-minded focus. We should make truth the single most dominant influence shaping our decisions and actions. We must let truth pervade our way of seeing and interpreting things and events. It then enables us to stick to what is good, sacred, and most importantly, real. This truth WILL set you free. Now, let's meditate on this.

Embracing the Truth That Will Set You Free Meditation

* *Begin by finding a comfortable and quiet space. Take a few deep breaths, allowing your body and mind to relax.*

* *As you settle into a calm state, bring your awareness to the concept of eternal truth. This truth is unwavering, unchanging, and universal. It transcends time, culture, and perspective. Truth guides us toward our divine nature.*

* *Contemplate the first aspect of eternal truth: its unchanging nature. This truth remains constant, even as*

the physical world around us changes. It is as relevant today as it was 5000 years ago and will continue to be so a million years from now. Allow the stability and consistency of eternal truth to bring a sense of comfort to your heart.

* *Now, consider the second aspect of eternal truth: its universality. Truth applies to every single person on the planet, regardless of their background, culture, or beliefs. Feel the interconnectedness that this truth creates among all human beings, and allow it to foster a sense of unity and compassion within you.*

* *Reflect upon the third aspect of eternal truth: its impartiality. It is the same from all perspectives and is not influenced by individual viewpoints. Recognize the beauty in this objective truth, free from bias or prejudice, and let it inspire you to seek unbiased understanding in your daily life.*

* *Finally, turn your attention to the fourth aspect of eternal truth: its power to reveal our divine nature. As you contemplate this eternal truth, allow it to guide you toward your inner divinity, a place of bliss and serenity that exists beyond the limitations of the senses.*

* *Bask in the light of this divine revelation, and experience the profound joy and freedom that comes from embracing eternal truth. Breathe in and out deeply, and with each breath, reaffirm your connection to this profound wisdom. You feel grounded and refreshed.*

6

WORLDVIEW MATTERS: HOW PERSPECTIVES SHAPE AND DRIVE OUR LIVES

What if you suddenly discovered your life is like a science fiction movie? In this scary movie, some strange creature inside you forces you to see things and treat people in a manner that doesn't align with your true will. Something like that is happening to us right now. That strange creature inside us is our unconscious, which is our irrational or unconsidered belief about the world and ourselves. Let's free ourselves and escape this horror. To do this, we need to shine a light on our worldview.

Worldview is usually defined as the lens through which we view our life and the world around us. We may inherit or create or discover these beliefs in any combination. These days most of us have mongrel worldviews. That is, our perception of reality is a mixture of inheritance, creation, and discovery.

You have a psychology whether or not you study psychology. Whether or not you contemplate your worldview, you have one. We all have value systems that are directly connected to our worldview. Everyone chooses to act in certain ways, revealing our values.

You are a person with free will that makes choices, even if it is simple things like getting out of bed in the morning, choosing whether and what to eat, or choosing to go to work. All these choices are based on values and a certain understanding of the world, even if we don't think or talk about it very much. So let's dig deep and see what is underpinning our lives and our choices. To understand our worldview better let's divide them into the following three categories:

1. Inside-out Worldview: What is inside us determines how we see and act in the world. Ralph Waldo Emerson said it best, "What lies behind you and what lies in front of you pales in comparison to what lies inside of you".

   In this inside-out worldview, we see that we are all one. All creatures of all races, all religions, and all nationalities, old and young, are all spiritually connected. We still notice different genders or religions but see the underlying unity of all beings. This is a transcendent worldview.

2. Outside-in Worldview: This worldview tells us that everything important in life is out there, and if our outside is okay, we will feel good inside. My relationships, my work, my position, my wealth, my appearance – that is what matters. The external is our only reference point for who we are. Our mind doesn't even consider an inner self. Most of us are invested in this worldview.

   In this worldview, we see different people, men or women or different races as really different. Men really are from Mars and women from Venus! Our differences are fundamental and final. Unlike the inside-out worldview, in this consciousness, we can't see past the differences.

3. Self-absorbed Worldview: In this worldview, we are so self-centered that we can't see past our immediate surroundings. We don't care about anyone or anything outside our inner circle. We only care about our work, job, and family in this state. We don't even have a sense of the world. We lose ourselves in a tiny, local reality.

SHINE A LIGHT ON YOUR WORLDVIEW AND EMBRACE THE SUBLIME

The most fundamental moral assumption of modern society is the equality of all people. However, that equality goes against all known empirical science. There is no conceivable empirical test that shows us to be equal. Everybody can't run as fast; everybody doesn't have the same IQ. Therefore, if we really are equal, our equality is based on our reality beyond the body. If you are a normal person and believe in some form of equality, if you believe in justice for all, then you are already committed (whether you know it or not) to a bi-dimensional worldview – physical but also metaphysical. In other words, you already believe in some spiritual reality beyond the body.

Why do we believe that the rich and poor get one vote? Why should the strong and the weak get equal justice before the law? Why must the Ph.D. and the high school dropout stop at the same red light? All these people, theoretically, have equal dignity under the law. But why? If you believe that we are all equal in some way, then you are already committed – consciously or unconsciously- to a spiritual worldview.

So, what is your worldview? Do you believe in equality? Are you against racism? Are you against sexism? Then you accept that we are all spiritual beings, and we are equal. Now that you are aware that you and everyone else are spiritual beings, let's bring this most important fact front and center in our lives and shine a light on it. For now, by "spiritual" we simply mean some core part of us that cannot be reduced to a mere physical machine existence.

Once you shine a light on your inner self, you may want to dust yourself off and be the best person you, the soul, can be. In other words, you may need to edit your life. You may see that there is a better way to live, feel, love, and make decisions that are free of unconscious, unworthy assumptions. You may want to reach higher and grab a better life. Let's bring the truth of ourselves into the open and see where it leads us.

What does this mean? Let's take a simple example – water. When we want to purify contaminated water and restore its sweet, clear, transparent nature, we remove everything that is not water. Similarly, if we remove from our worldview all that is not pure consciousness, our mind naturally becomes sublime and transparent. We see everything as it is. We see ourselves as we really are.

Adopt the Inside-Out Worldview and Revitalize Yourself

For Soul Fitness to work, we need to have the inside-out worldview as our dominant thought pattern. When we unconsciously possess either the outside-in or the self-absorbed worldviews, it leads to confusion and despair. This is because both those worldviews are false beliefs, and it's almost like a virus is invading and overtaking the soul.

If I want any spiritual experiences like love, happiness, liberty, peace, or security (yes, think about it, these are all spiritual experiences), then I should prescribe to the inside-out worldview. There should be intentionality about what we are thinking. My mind frame should consciously change.

As I mentioned, we all have a combination of the three worldviews. So let us purify our worldview. Let's burn off the cognitive fat. Let's remove the outside-in and self-absorbed worldviews from the soul. When you do this, you will not become someone else or something else. You will instead rediscover the real, pure, healthy you – a beautiful spiritual being.

EMBRACING THE INSIDE-OUT WORLDVIEW FOR SPIRITUAL GROWTH MEDITATION

* *Allow yourself to be still for a few moments. Just be here and now. Watch the body breathe.*

* *As you breathe, remind yourself that your inner world shapes your external experience. Reflect on Ralph Waldo Emerson's words: "What lies behind you and what lies in front of you pales in comparison to what lies inside of you".*

* *Visualize yourself adopting an inside-out worldview, where you recognize the interconnectedness of all beings. Imagine looking at the world and seeing beyond*

the differences in gender, religion, race, and nationality, acknowledging the underlying unity among us all.

* *In this meditative state, consider the spiritual experiences you desire, such as love, happiness, liberty, peace, and security. Recognize that by embracing the inside-out worldview, you open yourself to these experiences more fully.*

* *Now, set the intention to release any outside-in and self-absorbed worldviews that may be clouding your spiritual growth. Envision these false beliefs as a dark cloud, dissipating in the light of your newfound understanding.*

* *As you continue to breathe deeply, feel the purity and beauty of your true self emerging. With each breath, embrace your identity as a spiritual being, interconnected with all life.*

* *Take a moment to bask in the serenity and harmony that come from adopting the inside-out worldview. Gently bring your awareness back to your surroundings.*

* *Carry this purified worldview with you throughout your daily life, knowing that you have the power to shape your experiences and foster inner transformation through your thoughts and intentions.*

7

THE IMPORTANCE OF ASSUMPTIONS IN SPIRITUALITY

The Understanding Science site of the University of California at Berkeley says, "Much as we might like to avoid it, all scientific tests involve making assumptions — many of them justified." It goes on to give the example of a simple test of the hypothesis (the scientific word for assumption) that substance A inhibits bacterial growth is tested by comparing Petri dishes with substance A and an inert substance B, both mixed with growth medium. Bacteria are added, and the dishes are checked for colony growth after a day. The test relies on assumptions about the growth medium, substance B, the timeframe, and potential external influences. These assumptions are necessary as you must undergo this process to get results.

In both science and spirituality, we need assumptions as foundations for experimentation. Without practice, we won't gain experience or develop conviction. Like scientific laws that began as hypotheses and were confirmed through testing, spiritual principles also need testing. During the course of this book, we will take the time to test the following spiritual assumptions to arrive at the subsequent conclusion.

Spiritual Assumptions

1. I am a spiritual being having a human experience.
2. I am a being of peace, purity, love, bliss, and spiritual knowledge. These are my innate qualities.

Conclusion

YES! I am a soul and I feel blissful, powerful, and free.

Allow your mind to become a petri dish for spiritual exploration. In this case, the microbes are thoughts and ideas that influence our perception of reality. The first assumption you can make is that your true nature is love. This is a powerful starting point for any spiritual exploration. It is about understanding that we are beings of love, compassion, and kindness at our core.

Creating the right environment is crucial for your spiritual exploration. Just as a petri dish must be kept sterile and at the right temperature for microbes to grow, your mind must be calm and clear for spiritual insights to arise. This can be achieved through the Soul Fitness practices outlined in the subsequent chapters.

The meditation practice is our experiment. As you meditate, hold the assumption that your true nature is love. Let this thought be the seed that you plant in the petri dish of your mind. Cultivate it with your attention and care. Observe how it grows and influences your thoughts, feelings, and actions.

As with any experiment, patience and perseverance are key. But with time, you will find that your mind is indeed a fertile ground for spiritual growth. And your true nature of love will become apparent to you. This is the power of spiritual assumptions.

Your Intrinsic Nature Is Love Meditation

Within this meditation, we will seek to experience the truth that love is an innate aspect of our nature. It lies at the heart of who we are as sentient beings, waiting to be recognized and nurtured.

* *Breathe in and out slowly. Allow your body to relax.*

* *Direct your awareness toward the realm of your third eye. Imagine a radiant light glowing softly within it. This light represents the essence of love, your true nature. Allow this light to grow brighter and more vivid with each breath you take.*

* *As you breathe in, imagine this love making you feel whole. Now, visualize this love extending outwards, touching everyone around you. Feel the warmth and compassion that this love carries.*

* *Take a moment now and deeply reflect on how you are love. At your core, you have pure feelings, feelings of acceptance, and genuine respect for everyone.*

* *Remind yourself that this is a universal love that transcends all barriers, differences, and divisions. It is the love that connects all beings.*

* *Visualize this love as a golden thread weaving through the fabric of the universe, connecting your heart to the hearts of others.*

* *As you hold this image in your mind, remember that this love is not something external that you need to seek. It is already within you. It is your very nature, your essence.*
* *Hold onto this image of you being a radiant light of love and that you are connected to all beings. Carry this image with you, even as you return to your day.*

**Access free meditations to go deeper
into your quest for immortality:**

These Soul Fitness meditations will pave the way for your true spiritual nature to unfold, illuminate, and spread joy to yourself and the world.

Go here to get access now:

shireenchada.com/soulfitness

8

THE POWER OF ACCEPTANCE IN SPIRITUAL TRANSFORMATION

This is what I mean by acceptance - The act of assenting to (or favorably receiving) a set of assumptions. Acceptance means that we bring our assumptions out and shine a light and say to them, "I see you; I accept you because it is going to make a difference in my life.". It is getting in touch with our spiritual reality.

We should acknowledge that all that we perceive as true could be ingrained assumptions we've accepted unconsciously. Acceptance doesn't necessarily mean that we have blind faith or that this acceptance must continue indefinitely. It just means for now; I will suspend my disbelief.

As I mentioned in the last chapter, working assumptions (hypotheses) constitute a significant part of science. It is difficult to talk for long with a scientist about science without hearing the words, "If we assume". To make sense of things, we usually have to make assumptions, which help structure our thinking. Hence when we wholeheartedly accept our assumptions, we will have an increased level of understanding - In our case, experiences.

When you accept with your whole heart, you inevitably find the truth of your being. Finding the truth of your being provides a framework for your conviction. It provides validation of your true spiritual identity. People think of faith as if it were a strange activity, suitable only for people like Mother Teresa and Nelson Mandela. I want you to think of faith as an essential transformative technique. A tool we should all have in our toolkit to have transcendental experiences.

You wouldn't say, "I got a really good night's sleep last year, so it doesn't matter if I didn't get any last night.". We all know that the past, no matter how good it may once have been, is not of much use to us now. Why do we not create amazing experiences for ourselves every day, hour, and moment? Living and experiencing the original qualities of the soul is possible – all we have to do is accept the two assumptions and start doing the exercises in this book.

We sometimes feel we are more than these physical bodies. Now, let us fully accept this concept with determination: Yes, I am a soul and currently partaking in a human adventure! Bring this to the forefront of the mind. This simple shift in awareness transforms our lives because our awareness determines our state of being. If I'm aware that I am a spiritual being, then I gradually move to a higher state of being. When I believe with total acceptance, my awareness transforms me, the soul.

If you're still unsure about embracing acceptance, here are a few more reasons to consider:

- Any personal transformation requires some amount of effort and discipline on our part. Our minds don't want to put in that effort unless it realizes the importance of why we need to transform. For this, we require acceptance of the assumptions.

- I need to concentrate not so much on what needs to be changed in the world as on what needs to be transformed within myself. For me, the courage to change means focusing on how to bring about self-transformation. For any amount of transformation in our lives, we need acceptance.

- This kind of acceptance is empowering and practicing it will heal the self

- We want to control everything in our lives, but is that really possible? When I accept that I can only control my thoughts, which then brings about a certain awareness, my attitude changes and my vision and actions change.

- Paradoxically, this kind of acceptance makes you lighter! As soon as you stare at your assumptions in the face and think to yourself, "Okay, these are what I have to work with . . ." Then you feel like half the work is already accomplished.

Difference Between Blind Faith and Acceptance

Most people equate acceptance with blind faith. "If I accept things then it means I'm giving up my reasoning." But in reality, every single one of us accepts a set of subconscious assumptions. For example, do you accept Darwin's Theory of Evolution? Do you accept that the world was created in seven days by God? Do you accept that time, the world, and human beings are cyclic? If you answered yes to one of them, then you have accepted certain assumptions (knowingly or unknowingly). All of us accept something or other that we haven't personally empirically measured.

9

DISCOVERING WHO I AM AS CONSCIOUSNESS

As I mentioned earlier, at the heart of Soul Fitness is the idea that similar to a body's inherent healthy state, there is a natural, nourishing condition for the soul. Therefore, Soul Fitness requires that you know who you are and have a strong sense of your true self. As discussed in the previous chapter, most of us have bought into the outside-in worldview. That is, if we are content with our relationships, our work, our appearance, and our wealth, we believe we will be happy. Our mind is trained to look outside our true selves to fulfil our deepest needs, and our external identity becomes our main reference point for who we are.

This worldview stems from thinking we are physical beings searching for a spiritual experience. We believe that we are just a body with a heart and a mind. For Soul Fitness to work, we must embrace the inside-out worldview. It is essential to recognize that we are fundamentally spiritual beings encased in a human body.

I'd like to stress here that to grasp and implement Soul Fitness, we must learn the difference between consciousness and matter. Matter has physical properties such as volume, density, mass, size, etc. On the other hand, the attributes of consciousness include things like awareness, memory, creativity, reasoning, decision-making ability, thinking, observation, intuition, opinions, imagination, abstract thinking, etc.

The difference between matter and consciousness is most apparent at the moment of death when consciousness separates from matter. The body dies, and it stops functioning. But what happens to the conscious person who expressed themselves and experiences life through the body? It is commonly said, "The person has passed on." So, who passes on? You, the spiritual being, will pass on. When the conscious soul leaves the body, the body becomes a non-functioning corpse. So, who are you? You are consciousness itself. Other terms for consciousness are soul; the animating force; the conscious self; *atma*; the sentient being; the psyche and the spirit to give it a few names.

Visualizing the Soul as Light

So how can you conceive of yourself if you are not the body? Historically, Eastern and Western faiths have denoted consciousness or the soul as light. The soul is metaphysical light, that is, the soul is invisible to the physical eyes, but we visualize it as light. With our mind's eye, the third eye, we "see" the soul as a star or a point of light. The form of the soul is a tiny, conscious star of spiritual (metaphysical) light energy that the physical eyes cannot see. There are different ways of meditating in many other traditions that have been passed on to us for millennia. Here, in Soul Fitness, we are going to utilize this very powerful technique of visualization that really works.

Are you thinking – what a strange thought. For so long, you have thought of yourself as female or male or this or that particular race and now you are asked to think of yourself as a light. Yes, it is strange to begin with but the more you think deeply about this and the more you do the exercises in this book, you will become aware of yourself as a spiritual luminous being, full of life and experiences.

Exploring the Location of the Soul

We will meditate on the soul within the brain to harness our mental and intellectual powers. We will thus locate the soul deep inside the brain, in a place aligned with the space between, and slightly above the eyebrows.

This is a valuable technique for Soul Fitness, especially to get control of our thoughts and give us a point of focus. When we realize the soul is in that location, we gain direct power over our thoughts. A big part of Soul Fitness is to discipline the mind. Hence, visualizing the soul deep inside the brain helps you make your mind your friend and not your enemy.

The soul is a separate entity from the brain. The brain is the command center of our body/vehicle and the soul is the commander, the driver. Technically speaking the soul occupies no space in the physical body since it is not physical, but we are "seated," so to speak, deep inside the brain, behind the eyes. Our role as souls is to animate and "drive" the body via the brain and nervous system. This specific form of meditation has worked wonders in my own life. You will find it to be a powerful tool to gain a clear image of your spiritual self and a point of focus for your conscious life.

IMMORTALITY OF THE SOUL

Because the soul is spiritual energy, nothing physical can destroy it. No fire nor water, bullets, nor bombs can touch the soul. This means that you, the soul, have always existed and always will. The soul is immortal. The soul does not die. This means that you and I have always existed and always will. As it is metaphysical, there is nothing physical that can do away with it. The soul can neither be created nor destroyed. However, the soul is conscient and intelligent; consequently, the soul can absorb ideas, influences, and qualities.

Even though the soul is indivisible and indestructible, its quality and strength are subject to change. We will extensively use immortality of the soul throughout the book to regain total Soul Fitness.

In essence, we have forgotten who we are. This lack of awareness of one's true self causes the mind to mop the figurative floor and absorb sorrow, emptiness, and the grime of confusion. The soul tries to end these feelings with irrational sensual desires.

However, any happiness experienced through the physical senses is only temporary. To experience true Soul Fitness, I must remember who I truly am in all my glory.

Let's do a simple meditation to cement the above ideas in our psyche.

THE POWER OF SELF-REALIZATION MEDITATION

* *Slowly breathe in and out as you move deeper into your center. With each breath, allow yourself to go deeper and deeper into that quiet center within. Imagine that deep inside you there is a switch that can turn off all the chatter and noise of the mind. Turn this switch off now and relax into deep stillness.*

* *Now, bring your awareness to the space between and slightly above your eyebrows, deep within your brain. This is the location where we will visualize the soul. Repeat silently, "I am a luminous point of light."*

* *Take a moment now and visualize yourself as a tiny, luminous star, a being of light inside your forehead. You understand you are this light, you are invisible to the physical eyes, but with your mind's eye, your third eye, you can perceive yourself. You, the soul, this light, are pure and radiant.*

* *As you focus on yourself as a point of light, acknowledge that you, the soul, are separate from your brain. The brain is merely the command center of your body, while the soul is the driver, the true commander of your thoughts and actions. Realize that as you connect with yourself as a soul, you gain spiritual power.*

* *Allow the knowledge of the soul's eternal nature to fill you with a sense of serenity and peace. You, the soul, are*

metaphysical and immortal. You always exist and always will. You, the soul, cannot be created or destroyed.

- *As you meditate, understand and accept yourself as a soul. You are more than just your physical body. You are an eternal being of spiritual energy.*

- *Allow this awareness to seep into your consciousness, helping you to make your mind your friend and not your enemy. With each breath, connect with yourself as a soul. Keep repeating, "I am a soul, and I have a body". "I'm not the body; I'm a beautiful being of metaphysical light."*

- *Slowly begin to bring your awareness back to the room around you. Carry the sense of peace and inner strength you've cultivated during this meditation with you as you continue your journey toward Soul Fitness.*

10

DISCOVERING THE FOUNTAIN OF YOUTH THROUGH SOUL FITNESS

For millennia, people have searched for the Fountain of Youth, magical waters capable of reversing aging. Explorers traveled far to find these sacred, restorative waters. Modern explorers focus on medical science – but the goal is the same.

I will share a secret with all the scientists and billionaires who want immortality. It is possible -- through Soul Fitness. Soul Fitness doesn't just put a bandage on mortality concerns. It empowers you to see and be who you really are, an eternal, un-aging soul. Is it really worth all the trouble? Are you thinking since we all have to die at some point, why bother? Wait! Before you cave into mortality, I want you to truly experience immortality. Then decide after you've tasted it.

Embracing your true soul identity and seeing beyond the body is the first step in discovering your fountain of youth. So, let's start by learning what soul identity is:

- You actually see yourself as a soul.

- You know beyond doubt that you are a vibrant, eternal spirit.
- You realize that you, the soul, are the life force of your body.
- You experience your eternal qualities such as transcendent peace, purity, love, bliss, and wisdom.

Body identity on the other hand is to mistakenly take the physical body to be our true self. In this mistaken consciousness, we identify the self, the soul, with the body and its labels – race, gender, nationality, age, etc. You, the soul, must make the most important decision of your life. Will you choose to think of yourself as an aging, dying body or as an eternal un-aging soul? The body itself doesn't think. You, the soul, think within the body, using the body's neurological apparatus. You, the soul, will either see your true self or a false aging so-called self. We can therefore conclude that body identity means:

- You are conscious only of your physical-ness.
- You forget your spiritual identity and embrace a temporary nationality, gender, race, and age as yourself. You become your body's labels.
- You seek pleasure in the external world through the body's physical senses.

Over the course of many lifetimes, we dig ourselves deeper and deeper into body identity, and we rely more and more on the bodily senses as our only source of experience, knowledge, and pleasure. As we all know, in the physical world, everything changes and ultimately comes to an end. So as our pleasure derived from sense experiences diminishes, we get caught up in a negative feedback loop of desire and dependency on external stimuli. Lust, anger, greed, ego, and attachment take control. Body identity becomes the root of all our sorrow as the soul takes on these qualities.

We impose on others the same illusion. That is, we accept and reject others according to their bodily labels of gender, race, nationality, faith, profession, age, etc. Labeling hides the soul. Let's do a meditation to peel off these labels.

MEDITATION ON RELEASING LIMITING LABELS AND EMBRACING YOUR TRUE POTENTIAL

* *Find a comfortable position. Tense your face muscles tightly, then relax and breathe. Next, tense the muscles in your chest, arms, and hands; hold and release as you breathe. Repeat this for your legs and feet. Finally, tense your entire body, hold the tension, and relax. Breathe and feel your muscles loosen, preparing to enter a space of light.*

* *Begin by acknowledging the labels you have acquired over the course of many lifetimes. These labels may be related to your nationality, gender, race, or social status. Recognize how these labels may have limited your potential and led you to sorrow by preventing you from experiencing your true essence.*

* *Now, imagine these labels as chains that have bound you, keeping you from realizing your full potential. With each*

deep breath, imagine the chains breaking apart, one by one, as you free yourself from their constraints.

* *As you release these labels, feel the weight of centuries of cultural baggage lifting off your shoulders. Embrace the freedom of simply being a soul, unencumbered by any limiting identity.*

* *With each breath, allow yourself to reconnect with your innate virtues – honesty, justice, self-esteem, goodness, and a sense of noble purpose. Feel the warmth of these virtues filling your entire being, empowering you to see beyond the limitations of your bodily labels.*

* *Take a few more deep breaths, allowing this newfound freedom to sink in.*

* *Carry this knowledge with you as you continue your life's journey, free from the limitations of labels and full of love, peace, and virtue.*

Hypnotized by Labels: Breaking Free from Body Identity

A hypnotherapist hypnotized a man into thinking he was a buffalo. When this man was fully convinced he was a buffalo, he was asked to leave the room. He responded, "How can I leave the room? I'm a buffalo and won't fit through the door?"

The story illustrates how we hypnotize ourselves over the course of many lifetimes into identifying with bodily "labels" and the limitations that come with those labels. These labels limit us from realizing our true potential. For example, if I think I'm an Indian female, then centuries of cultural baggage surrounding the Indian female weigh me down, and I won't realize my full potential. Seeing myself through the lens of body identity leads me to sorrow.

Here is a comparison of qualities arising from different states of awareness

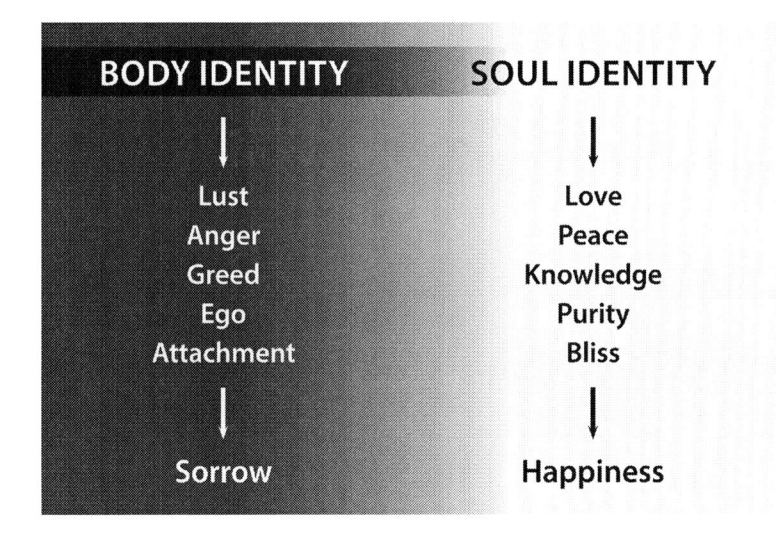

BODY IDENTITY	SOUL IDENTITY
↓	↓
Lust	Love
Anger	Peace
Greed	Knowledge
Ego	Purity
Attachment	Bliss
↓	↓
Sorrow	Happiness

There are many vices and virtues beyond the five mentioned above. But these are primary. Fortunately, the virtues are innate to the soul, so it is natural to revive them. How do we know this?

Just as we would never crave food that we never tasted, similarly, if love, peace, and happiness were not part of our inherent make-up, we wouldn't desire them. We seek virtues because they are inherent to our souls. When we feel good, we feel natural and never seek to become unhappy.

Why do we react so strongly against dishonesty or injustice? Because we want to experience the original virtues of honesty and justice. We intuitively know that our deep well-being rests on virtues such as self-esteem, goodness, and a sense of noble purpose. Giving gifts and giving ourselves to a higher purpose is natural for us, as evidenced by numerous studies in Positive Psychology. These studies show us that we can't be happy unless we share, unless we give. Hence, our innate nature is virtuous, it is love, it is peace.

STEPS TO DISCOVERING THE FOUNTAIN OF YOUTH

The first step is understanding that eternal youth is within us. The second step is to see ourselves as unageing souls and to keep that light of awareness switched on. We accomplish this simply by the spiritual fitness workout of repeatedly remembering that we are souls. I've included fifty exercises in this book to help you achieve this sublime consciousness.

I always tell the participants in my courses that there is a three-step formula to becoming soul aware. 1. Practice 2. Practice 3. Practice. Everything depends on practicing the exercises in this book. Remember -- you can change your consciousness at any moment, even right in the middle of an action. The exercises are deliberately designed to teach you to be soul aware amid the action. When we fail to practice, the awareness light is switched off. If we're attentive, we can create the thoughts necessary to experience the fountain of youth. It takes time and practice to change something that has been 'normal' our whole life. We need patience and determination. Let's do a meditation to switch on our soul identity.

The Fountain of Youth Within: Journeying to Your Radiant Soul Identity Meditation

* *Sit comfortably and place your feet flat on the ground slightly apart. Sit up allowing your spine to be straight and comfortable. Take a deep breath and relax in a quiet space deep inside your being.*

* *As you continue breathing, imagine yourself as an explorer seeking the fountain of youth. Instead of searching for physical waters, embark on a journey within yourself.*

* *Now, take a moment to visualize your true spiritual identity. See yourself as a radiant, eternal soul, a vibrant spirit that exists beyond the confines of your physical body.*

* *As you explore your true identity, begin to recognize that you are the life force animating your body.*

* *With each breath, allow yourself to experience your eternal qualities. Feel the transcendent peace that exists within you as it washes over your entire being like a soothing waterfall. Let it cleanse you, purifying your thoughts and emotions.*

* *Now, focus on the love that dwells within your soul. Feel it expand and envelop your entire being, connecting you to every other soul on this planet. Experience the warmth of this love, knowing that it is an unbreakable bond that transcends time and space.*

* *At this moment, recognize that your search for the Fountain of Youth has led you to your true self – an immortal soul. You now understand that immortality is not about*

> *escaping death but about embracing the eternal nature of you, the spirit.*
>
> * *Take a few more deep breaths, allowing this realization to sink in. When you are ready, gently open your eyes, bringing your newfound awareness back into the world.*
>
> * *You have discovered the true Fountain of Youth within yourself. Embrace your eternal nature and live each day as a vibrant, un-aging soul filled with peace, purity, love, bliss, and wisdom.*

11

THE JOURNEY WITHIN: UNLEASHING THE HERO IN YOU THROUGH THOUGHTS

The well-known adage, "Cogito, ergo sum" or "I think, therefore I am" highlights the significance of our thoughts in defining our existence as spiritual entities. The critical impact of thoughts on molding us and directing us toward Soul Fitness cannot be understated. In this chapter, we will delve into the intricacies of thoughts through The Hero's Journey.

The media constantly presents us with The Hero's Journey, featuring countless "heroes" overcoming challenges to return victorious. This narrative captivates us because it reflects our challenges in understanding and regaining our true selves. Being a Soul Fitness hero requires the courage to recognize your spiritual and emotional shortcomings, and the determination and perseverance to comprehend your thoughts to focus on those that uplift your soul. Your progress in this book demonstrates your commitment to this heroic endeavor.

As spiritual fitness heroes, let's delve into our thoughts, confront the challenges, and attain our inner treasures. To progress, we must break free from the mundane and have the courage to pursue our purpose.

A six-stage journey of self-discovery will reveal new perspectives of our true selves, the soul.

STAGE 1: INITIATION INTO THOUGHTS

Some people speculate that we have 30 to 50 thousand thoughts daily. If that is even roughly accurate, it's a lot of thoughts. This means that our life is largely made up of thoughts. And those thoughts determine the quality of our life. In fact, we can never really not think; the mind is constantly busy.

A thought is a mental picture, a word, an idea, an opinion, or a sequence of ideas forming an argument. Thought is energy. The mind doesn't exist without some thought or the other. Thoughts are food for the mind, and just like with physical fitness when we feed our mind good, nutritious thoughts, we have a healthy consciousness. If we feed the mind toxic and junk thoughts, then the mind becomes toxic, unhappy, and sick. It is not enough to feed our minds nutritious thoughts once in a while. But honestly, how often do we give our minds a nutritious feast of good thoughts?

Thoughts become mental habits that we follow automatically. We often think without being truly aware. At times this becomes daydreaming. We need to understand our thoughts because they govern almost everything in our lives. Let's delve into what makes a thought a dragon, a friend, or a treasure.

Stage 2 – Slay the Dragon of Negative Thoughts

Our negative thoughts are like the proverbial dragon that needs to be slayed. Negative thoughts such as fear, despair, and ego harm us because these thoughts make us feel hopeless, worthless and lose touch with reality. Many of us may want to help others and do good for the world, but we must first slay the dragon of negative thoughts within ourselves. We can't avoid or postpone this fight. We must do it, and we must do it now.

Stage 3 – Know the Familiar Foe of Useless Thoughts

Thoughts that leave us discontented or confused are useless, and these thoughts are like the familiar foe. We know these thoughts are there and we even entertain them, but we must end these thoughts to get to the treasure. If we feed this foe of useless thoughts, then it takes control of us by making us obsessive and compulsive. It will never let us go. We must free ourselves. We often fall victim to this foe when we are bored. This foe weakens us spiritually and sucks our enthusiasm.

Stage 4 – Transcend the Status Quo of Mundane Thoughts

Ordinary thoughts are our status quo. These are not necessarily negative or wasteful, but are simply mundane - thoughts about work, paying bills, and dealing with the myriad relationships and duties that structure our lives. We cannot avoid these duties. But remember why you are reading this book. You want something more in life. You want it, and you know you are capable of experiencing magic. You, the hero, the soul, don't really belong in a humdrum life. You are destined for greatness. Don't be satisfied with the ordinary.

STAGE 5 – BE GUIDED BY YOUR FRIEND (POSITIVE THOUGHTS)

Your thoughts are positive and act as your friends when based on courage, honesty, and faith. Positive thoughts uplift us. An example of a positive thought based on faith is: I believe I can have a great life. An example of a positive thought based on courage is: I have strength and courage; I will not give up when I'm feeling low. We need this friend (positive thoughts). On the journey to rediscovering our true selves, this friend is invaluable. But we shouldn't mistakenly think these thoughts are the treasure itself. Positive thoughts are friends that help us find the treasure.

STAGE 6 – FIND THE ULTIMATE TREASURE: PURE, ETERNAL THOUGHTS FOR SOUL FITNESS

Pure, eternal thoughts about the original self are our ultimate treasure. This treasure, pure thoughts, creates a powerful awareness that transforms our lives and makes us heroes. These thoughts make us healthy, whole, and elevated. An example of a treasure-thought that is simple but powerfully transformative— I am a soul experiencing life through a human form. That is, I'm an eternal soul encased in a temporary material body. The amazing thing about this treasure is that it is self-generative. When we know the treasure, our mind can produce and reproduce it! Knowing the treasure helps us slay the dragon of negativity and reconnect with our true, luminous selves. This treasure illuminates our life and every life we touch.

Pure, eternal thoughts create a powerful awareness that elevates us, just as intense training and proper nutrition can elevate our physical performance. And just as we need to maintain our physical fitness with consistent effort, we must continue to nourish our minds with these pure thoughts to maintain our spiritual fitness.

In the end, the journey of rediscovery is to silence the mind through elevated and eternal thoughts of the pure self. These powerful thoughts quieten the mind. How does this happen? Pure thoughts come straight from the soul, relieving all our anxiety, and soothing the anxious, troubled mind. Such thoughts bring clarity and stillness.

Here is a recap of what constitutes an eternal thought. For a concept or thought to be considered eternal, it must meet the following criteria:

- It remains unchanged over time, meaning it's the same today, 5000 years ago, and a million years in the future.
- It applies equally to all people worldwide, regardless of their background or circumstances.

- It is consistent from all perspectives, maintaining its truth regardless of the observer.
- Upon reflection, it unveils our divine nature, leading us to experience a transcendent state of divinity and bliss beyond the senses.

Awakening the Spiritual Fitness Hero Meditation

* *Let go of the world of struggle. Allow yourself to relax and release any subtle forms of "trying to make anything happen." Breathe in and out at your own natural pace. Notice the breath as it passes in and out... in and out... Sense the breath moving through you as you relax into the moment.*

* *Now, envision yourself as a spiritual fitness hero, journeying deep into the realm of your thoughts. You're on a quest to confront the metaphorical dragon and seize the treasure it protects, bringing it back to your world.*

* *Visualize a path before you, leading you to spiritual riches. Feel the courage to break away from your comfort zone and pursue your treasure.*

* *See yourself going deeper and deeper into the path. With each step, you discover new perspectives of yourself as a soul. You gently realize that pure, eternal thoughts of your original self are the ultimate treasure.*

* *Allow the treasure of pure thoughts to generate a potent awareness that transforms your life. Feel these thoughts make you healthy, complete, and uplifted.*

* *Now, repeat the following affirmation in your mind: "I am a soul experiencing life through a human form—an eternal soul housed within a temporary material body."*

* *Again, repeat silently, "I am a soul experiencing life through a human form—an eternal soul housed within a temporary material body." You are beginning to experience a stillness and a joy beyond the senses. Feel the power of this stillness helping you vanquish the dragon of negativity, reconnecting with your true, radiant self.*

* *Allow the light of the soul to guide you as you journey through life as a spiritual fitness hero. When you feel ready, gently bring your awareness back to the present moment.*

12

SOUL FITNESS WARM-UPS: EASING INTO YOUR SPIRITUAL JOURNEY

My motto is, "When in doubt, do a warm-up." These gentle yet effective exercises are designed to ease you into the more demanding Soul Fitness regimen. Essential for preparing your mind for deeper mental activity, they enhance your willingness to engage in the rest of the exercises in this book. It's important to be firm yet gentle with yourself, maintaining discipline when nurturing your spiritual well-being.

These warm-ups will leave you feeling receptive and primed for your Soul Fitness journey, helping to loosen up your mental muscles. Before delving deeper into the book, try one or more exercises to set the stage for a rewarding experience. I've organized them progressively, starting with the easier ones and gradually moving to more challenging tasks. Regardless of your current level, include these warm-up exercises as a fundamental component of your Soul Fitness routine.

ENHANCED *SHAVAASANA*: A JOURNEY TO SELF-AWARENESS

Renowned hatha yogis say that *Shavaasana*, or the corpse (*shava*) pose (*asana*), is one of the most important *asanas*. Our exercise here enhances the traditional *shavaasana*, for we make a conscious decision to relax, de-clutter the mind, surrender to the moment, and become aware of our original self.

- Find a quiet spot and sit or lay down comfortably. Put your phone on airplane mode, and leave no scope for distractions. Relax your arms by your side. Keep your spine straight and your legs extended and slightly apart.

- Breathe in and out naturally.

- Close your eyes, focus your mind on your feet, feel in them the light of spiritual energy; tense them up for a couple of seconds, then let them go. Your feet should feel heavy now. Visualize this light energy coming up to your ankles. Focus your mind on your ankles, feel spiritual energy (light) in them, tense them up for a few seconds, and then let them go. Your feet and ankles should feel relaxed now. Let the light energy travel up to your lower legs. Now do the same with your lower legs, thighs, hips, stomach, chest, shoulder, arms, neck, face, and head. Your whole body should completely relax. While you progress up your body, visualize the light energy traveling up through your body.

- Now, focus your light energy in the center of your forehead. There is a powerful feeling of centeredness.

- Now, become aware of yourself as light, a luminous star in the center of the forehead. This star is you, the life force of your body.

- Invite peace and balance to enter you. Remain aware of yourself as light and silently say, "I am peace. I am peace."

Soul Fitness Breathing:
A Holistic Approach to Reducing Stress

Just a few minutes of observing the self while the body breathes can relax you and reduce your stress. This exercise can be done anywhere, anytime in a meeting, when your spouse is yelling at you or cooking. Here's how to do it:

- Meditate on your breath going in and out of the body.
- Lower your eyes slightly and through the corners of your eyes, watch your shoulders go up and down as the body breathes.
- Go a little bit deeper and become aware of yourself as a soul in the body.
- You are the animating force, the spiritual energy, the soul in the center of the forehead.
- From the vantage point of being a soul, peacefully observe the body as air flows in and out, in and out, in and out of it.
- Deepen your breath and continue to watch the body breathe.

HEALING YOUR BODY WITH LIGHT

This warm-up exercise is designed to guide you to relaxation, healing, and self-love. As you follow the steps, you'll be imagining soothing light energy flowing through you, cleansing your body and the soul, and ultimately cultivating a profound sense of serenity and balance.

- Find a comfortable position and maintain a soft gaze with your eyes partially closed. Take deep breaths and with each exhale, relax your body until you feel entirely at ease.

- Visualize a soothing light starting from the top of your head and moving down to your feet. As it traverses, imagine it cleansing, healing, and bringing harmony to each part of your body it touches.

- Extend this healing light into the earth, imagining it carrying away all negative energies from your body, leaving you feeling lighter and purified.

- Take a deep breath, feeling a sense of wholeness and healing within yourself. Hold this feeling for as long as you can.

- In this state of self-awareness, visualize another light, filled with pure love, cascading down your body from head to feet. Feel it easing any hurt and pain and treat your body as sacred. Envision yourself becoming lighter, enveloped in a warm embrace of serenity and comfort.

THE POWER OF THOUGHT OBSERVATION

It is amazing what happens to your thoughts just by the simple act of observation! They start to slow down. When we say "thoughts", they could be an image, a word, an emotion, an idea, or a feeling. While doing this exercise, observe your thoughts. You don't have to share them, so don't judge them as bad or good or whatever else; just watch them as a spectator. Here's how to do it:

- Think of your bedroom - what is the first thing that comes up? Is it a visual image? Is it a feeling? Is it a word?

- Remember your last vacation – what are your thoughts about it?

- Now, visualize a white screen and note your first thought in response to the following words: War; Neighbor; Beach; Spouse.

- Keep observing your thoughts. When you walk into your home, your work, when you see certain people. Just be aware of them. Pick the first thought. What came to you?

- Remember not to judge your thoughts . . . they just are.

Free Your Mind: Escaping the Shackles of Negativity

In some parts of the world, people live in physical slavery. They are denied fundamental rights, like access to information, and are subjected to propaganda. In much the same way, we enslave our minds by thinking the same negative thoughts again and again and again.

This exercise will teach us to identify negative thinking and transform it into powerful positive thinking. The exercise will set our minds free of negative thoughts and contribute greatly toward mental agility and flexibility through positive thinking just as when you are physically fit, you can enjoy freedom of movement.

- Accept that you have the capacity to generate negative and positive thoughts. Silently say to yourself, "I recognize these two different kinds of thoughts. I will consciously choose positive thoughts."

- Remember a negative thought you've had in the last few days when you felt annoyance, stress, or sorrow. Identify the negative thought patterns, habits of thinking in a particular way, you had at that time.

- Now, think of an opposite positive thought. For example, if your negative thoughts were, "I'm terrible, I'm not worth much," switch it to "I am a good person. My life has great value." If you thought, "Why do bad things happen to me," switch it to, "I'm lucky. There is benefit in everything." If you thought, "Why am I not getting a break in life?" Switch it to: "Life is full of opportunities and I have unlimited potential. Success is my birthright. I know how to seize opportunities."

- Pick two reoccurring negative thoughts and practice your new positive thought every time that negative thought enters your mind.

- As the positive replacement thought pattern becomes a habit, the negative thought pattern will gradually disappear, and only the positive thought pattern will remain. Once you master this technique, you will find yourself naturally switching more negative thoughts into positive ones. You will unleash a domino effect of negative into positive.

- These mental stretches will help you explore the world and yourself. If you want mental agility, you must feed your mind with positive thoughts. This is a healthy diet and workout for the mind.

EMBODYING AN ATTITUDE OF GRATITUDE

Our attitudes and feelings are based on what we think. Hence, it is essential to become aware of our thoughts and to choose an attitude of gratitude. By choosing an attitude of gratitude, we choose the quality of life we want to lead.

- As soon as you wake up in the morning, become aware of your first few thoughts.
- Then, think of two things you are grateful for. It could be big, like your health, or it could be small, like, the air conditioning is still working.
- If this exercise doesn't work for you when you wake up, pick an activity you perform every day, like getting into the shower or sitting down for breakfast.
- Just before performing that activity, pick two things you are grateful for in your life. If you forget, go back to the beginning of the activity and do it. For example, if you picked sitting down for breakfast as your gratitude moment and forgot to be grateful, then get up (even in the middle of breakfast), remember your two grateful things in life, and then sit down to eat.

There is a lot of research done on the importance of gratitude. This simple exercise will perk up your life and your Soul Fitness.

HEALING THOUGHTS, HEALING SELF

This exercise covers healing your perception of yourself with a simple affirmative conversation. Psychology and many other fields are beginning to recognize that thoughts have energy. When the soul, the animating force of the body, has a thought, then the body first absorbs that energy because it is the closest to the soul. The body is the first environment in which the soul lives and operates. Hence, anything that the soul thinks is stored in the physical body. Therefore, it is essential to become aware of the inner workings of your mind and to choose healing thoughts for two reasons, 1. To heal the body, and 2. To heal the self, the soul.

- You have to accept that your thoughts will affect your body and your perception of yourself first and then others.

- Have a silent conversation with yourself, "I am a master, the creator of my thoughts. I always have a choice in what I think."

- Now, pick a negative or wasteful thought that you've had in the last few days, and visualize it being stored in the body. Ask yourself, "How did this thought affect my body?" "Which organ did it get stored in?" For example, heart or gut area or . . .

- Pick a diametrically opposite positive thought to the negative thought you've had. An example, "I'm stressed about my job. What if I lose it or don't get that promotion or . . ." Now, transform it by silently saying to yourself, "What is mine will always come to me. My needs will be fulfilled. I have everything I need to lead a balanced life."

- Remember stress and negativity directly impact the physical body. This Soul Fitness exercise directly improves our physical wellness.

REFRESH YOUR MIND, REVIVE YOUR SPIRIT

When we remember past moments of happiness, we feel refreshed, and our feelings change. When we relish memories of life's good things, they give us joy. Let us here discover how our own thoughts can refresh our minds and how recognizing beauty and goodness can refresh the mind.

- Find a quiet spot and sit quietly. For a few moments, stretch your mind. Go into a past experience and bring it into the present.

- Remember a time when you felt peace. It could be this year, this month, this week, or even in the last few minutes.

- What was that feeling? What was the experience? Where were you? What were you doing? Bring the whole experience to the forefront of your mind. Savor the experience again by reflecting on its details.

- Now connect with the feeling of peace within. Give yourself a few moments in this peaceful, serene state.

Your mind is slowing down, and you are beginning to be refreshed.

CREATING YOUR SERENITY PRAYER

We all have heard the serenity prayer, which goes like this:

God grant me the serenity to:
Accept the things I cannot change,
Have the courage to change the things I can,
And have the wisdom to know the difference.

Creating a customized serenity prayer for yourself is a fun and useful exercise. This prayer would reflect what you are going through in life right now.

- Pick a situation or person at work or in your personal life that is disturbing your peace.
- With courage, look within and see how you contribute to the situation. Remember, it always takes two hands to clap. Ask yourself the question, "What is it that needs to be transformed within myself."
- With understanding and peace, clearly see what you can do and what you cannot do in that situation. What is in your hands and what is not in your hands?
- Keep repeating to yourself silently, "I trust. I trust myself. I trust that when I transform, everything around me will transform. I trust this cosmic law. I trust this process will have a beneficial outcome."
- Now write your customized serenity prayer.

I am aware of the difference between what I can accomplish on my own, what I have to put in the hands of others, and what I have to leave up to destiny. I am at peace with that.

13

EASY SOUL FITNESS: STAGES ON THE JOURNEY

All humans desire love, peace, happiness, freedom, and enjoyment. However, when we attempt to obtain these things from the material world, it often enslaves us. Instead of achieving freedom, we become dependent. The most crucial form of freedom we need to focus on right now is liberating our minds. We must free our minds from the influence of self-sabotaging thought patterns and behaviors. By practicing the exercises in this book, you will learn to liberate yourself, allowing you to experience true freedom.

The journey to Soul Fitness comprises four distinct stages: understanding, centering, concentration, and experience. These stages represent the natural flow of consciousness when we engage our minds and intellects with spiritual concepts. Easy Soul Fitness is achieved by concentrating on an exercise, following a logical sequence of steps, and cherishing each step. In doing so, you will effortlessly connect with your inner divinity. This is the core principle of Soul Fitness.

Understanding: The First Stage on the Inner Journey

The first and most important aspect of having a powerful experience is understanding. We need to understand that we are so much more than these material bodies. Our greatness is so much more than just what meets the physical eye. Based on this understanding, then we accept. When understanding and acceptance are aligned, we can turn our attention within and become aware of our inner state. There is a whole universe inside the soul, and it is waiting to be discovered by you. When we focus inward, we engage our awareness, understanding, and acceptance and begin the journey.

- With understanding, I shift my identity to being a soul. A divine being, having a human existence.
- I focus my attention inside my forehead, behind my eyes, and have the thought, "This is where I sit."
- I select a single exercise and delve into it. For instance, if I am intrigued by the concept of being a spiritual traveler today, I will continue to investigate that particular concept until I gain a firm grasp on it.

Be aware of the initial struggle you may encounter with your mind at this stage. This happens because your consciousness is used to the material world, with its focus on external things. As a result, it may be scattered in various directions, causing this phase to take longer than anticipated. However, continue persevering until you become comfortable with the process. Ultimately, we can teach ourselves anything when we truly dedicate our hearts to it. Persistence will tame the restless mind, and soon enough, you will smoothly transition into the subsequent stage.

REFLECTION: THE SECOND STAGE ON THE INNER JOURNEY

This second stage of the journey is all about deep reflection. You reflect on being a soul. One by one, take up the exercises in the book and let them inform your mind. "I'm immortal. I'm a point of light, a being of peace. I'm the driver and this body is my vehicle."

Consider each exercise and thoughtfully go over them. "I am immortal.". "How do I feel about never dying?" "The essence of who I am will always live." All you are doing in this stage is remembering spiritual knowledge that is latent within you. Another effective way of deep reflection is asking yourself questions and focusing your mind on the answers. "What is spiritual love? How does it feel to experience spiritual love?" Questions help keep the mind in a state of reflection.

A wandering mind is an obstacle to Soul Fitness at this stage of the journey. All sorts of thoughts will appear important, ranging from "What should I have for dinner?" to "How could that person do that to me?" to "I forgot to take the trash out..." At this point, gently put a brake on these distractions and redirect them toward the exercise you are focusing on. Remind yourself, "For the next 30 minutes (or your chosen duration), I will concentrate on my inner self. I will devote my full attention to this later." Braking means halting any thoughts or analysis of the distraction, while redirecting involves using your intellect to refocus on the exercise.

It might be useful to keep a notepad to jot down things you suddenly remember and fear you may forget if you put it aside.

CONCENTRATION: THE THIRD STAGE ON THE INNER JOURNEY

Concentration implies the absence of extraneous thoughts. Once you have put aside distractions and begun to contemplate a specific exercise deeply, you start to concentrate. My recommendation is to focus on one exercise at a time. Here's what I do to aid my concentration:

I divide an exercise into three or four steps and proceed through them sequentially. The crucial aspect is to move through all the steps in order without any unrelated thoughts. If, after contemplating step two, you have an external thought for example, what's for dinner? you'll need to return to the first step and restart the sequence without any unnecessary or negative thoughts. Repeat this process until you can complete all the steps without stray thoughts. Engaging your visualization and comprehension abilities is essential when going through the steps. Cultivating understanding, visualization, and imposing a consequence for having unrelated thoughts will lead the soul to concentration.

For example, let's look at the exercise of you being eternal.

1. Waking up from the deep sleep of ignorance, I discover the true me. I'm a soul as subtle as a star. I'm real and conscious. I, the living star, am beyond age, beyond time.

2. I see myself as an eternal traveler through time. I've journeyed to this physical world and have gotten entangled in material things. I'm beyond time.
3. I feel like a timeless, ancient being moving through time and space with the help of this body. I'm a traveler. This isn't my permanent home.
4. In my eternal form, my light shines at its fullest capacity. I, the living star, am beautiful and wondrous.

Your ability to concentrate depends on how long you can focus on these steps in sequence without being distracted by external factors or other internal thoughts. If you don't experience it immediately, keep practicing. Think of it as a treadmill for the soul. This intentional exercise of the soul will lead you to experience yourself as an eternal soul.

This subtle transition from reflection to feeling is known as concentration. It occurs when the mind and intellect remain stable in a single consciousness. The longer you remember without distractions and let your thoughts align with an exercise, the more profound the experience of those thoughts will become.

EXPERIENCE: THE FOURTH STAGE ON THE INNER JOURNEY

The fourth stage, experience, is when you reach your destination. You embody the objective of an exercise, for instance, silence. You become still, and your inner faculties achieve total harmony. You attain a state of complete silence. If you haven't reached this stage yet, don't worry – with determination, anything is possible. Just keep practicing the concentration stage until you have experience.

As you start practicing, you may have some immediate experiences, while others may develop over time. The journey from understanding an aspect to deep reflection and finally to concentration is a return to something you already knew at the deepest level. By embodying the form of an exercise, it becomes deeply ingrained in the soul and leaves an imprint.

When you engage in one or more of the exercises in this book, it initiates long-term and possibly permanent changes within the soul. Your inherent nature will begin to manifest in your life. The more exercises you complete, the easier it becomes to restore your original essence. The game-changer here is the ability to build spiritual equity. The more exercises you do, the more transcendent experiences you can accumulate, like a spiritual savings account. Similar to any savings account, it's ideal to begin as soon as possible – there's no better time than the present! Your consciousness always remembers. It's not far-fetched to expect your original divine core to resurface when you practice even one exercise.

14

UNCOVERING THE PRIMARY QUALITIES OF THE SOUL

I distinguish between primary qualities and virtues in this book and our exercises. Primary qualities are five and they include love, peace, purity, bliss, and knowledge. Virtues represent combinations of primary qualities, such as simplicity, determination, courage, freedom, acceptance, introversion, and discipline. For an in-depth exploration of virtues, refer to my book, *Oh My Goodness! Grow Your Virtues and Flourish*.

Primary qualities are innate to the soul and can be combined to form a wide range of virtues, similar to how primary colors can be mixed to create a diverse palette of colors visible to the human eye. Analogously, all virtues can be derived by blending the five primary qualities.

The ultimate goal of Soul Fitness is to experience these qualities. To do so, we require a thorough understanding of the different elements—what they are, how they function, and how to apply them in our lives. A comprehensive grasp of the soul's primary qualities is crucial to truly feeling and living them.

Love: A Journey Toward Wholeness

Love is an intensely tender and ardent feeling directed toward another individual. It encompasses a profound sense of affection, as experienced towards a parent, child, or friend. And St. Paul in the Corinthians said, "Love is patient, love is kind. It does not envy; it does not boast; it is not proud. It does not dishonor others, it is not self-seeking, it is not easily angered, and it keeps no record of wrongs. Love does not delight in evil but rejoices with the truth. It always protects, always trusts, always hopes, and always perseveres."

In my experience, love resembles a multifaceted diamond. Although the various aspects of a diamond contribute to its beauty, there is still a single diamond at its core. Similarly, a primary quality like love possesses numerous facets that come together to form a beautifully unified emotion. This cohesive sentiment is typically expressed toward another individual.

The following aspects, among others, are the different facets of love.

- Friendship - True love in friendship arises from sharing one's authentic self and trusting deeply.

- Respect - Genuine love respects and values another for their innate goodness.

- Generosity - Limitless, unconditional love is characterized by noble generosity. Silently and freely giving to others without seeking credit exemplifies this expansive love.

- Acceptance - Embracing others as they are demonstrates selflessness and pure appreciation.
- Belonging - Love fosters a sense of belonging and security, empowering us to overcome challenges and achieve the impossible.
- Detachment - True love balances deep affection with healthy detachment, promoting unbiased freedom and lasting happiness.
- Affection - Expressing pure feelings and care through small gestures, cool-headed responses, and warm-hearted interactions embodies affectionate love.

In conclusion, love serves as a unifying force that connects souls. By intertwining our purest feelings from the heart with another, we experience a sense of wholeness, completion, and strength. As clichéd as it may sound, the truth remains that you and I are one. We are meant to be together, and we bring each other into existence through pure, genuine love.

PEACE: EMBRACING SOULFUL SERENITY

Inner peace is a state of tranquility, serenity, and harmony within the soul. The absence of internal disturbances, conflicts, or turmoil characterizes it. The soul experiences serenity, exuding a sense of satisfaction and harmony within oneself.

There are two ways to experience inner peace:

1. When the soul detaches from the body, the sense organs of the body, and stabilizes in being a soul, then we can touch inner peace.

2. When we become aware of ourselves as souls and reflect on peace.

I've devoted Chapter 24 to several exercises for the first method. Now, let's reflect on peace.

Originally, my nature is peace. Peace was a natural part of my life, and I've lost that inner peace. Like, love, peace is a single feeling, but it also constitutes many aspects. Some of them are:

- Serenity - An inner state of calmness, free from disturbances in thoughts and feelings, reflecting mastery over one's mind.

- Contentment - Stemming from satisfaction with one's possessions and inner self, trusting in the fulfilment of one's needs, and feeling a sense of fullness. Contentment is the most sacred aspect of peace.

- Harmony - Achieved through the alignment of my inside and outside lives.

- Balance - Found by maintaining the middle ground between pairs of positive qualities, such as love and detachment.
- Quietness - Attained by mastering a stable, still, and silent mind, leading to a peaceful life.
- Tranquility - Characterized by a refreshing and relaxing atmosphere in physical spaces and relationships.

Peace is an original quality of the self. Without experiencing peace, we can't experience love. Peace is everything. I don't let a day go by without connecting with my core quality of peace. Peace is my strength. When I am at peace, I am truly at one with myself. In my life, peace is the most sacred point of reference. I will not allow myself to lose it or forget it. I always think, "I have such peace that it is as if the earth, sky, and everything belongs to me."

Purity: Restoring the Soul's Innocence

In its natural, original state, consciousness is pure and untainted by vices such as lust, anger, greed, ego, and attachment. Purity leads to happiness and, unlike love and peace, is a singular, unambiguous attribute of the soul. Achieving purity involves eliminating vices, illusions, and deceptions from the soul, restoring it to a state of innocence akin to a newborn baby. In this state, there are no thoughts of causing harm or corruption and no traces of illusions or deceptions. Thus, absolute purity is attained when vices no longer influence our thoughts. Are you wondering how this is possible? If we can accept and have conviction, then we can accomplish it.

So, what are the convictions underpinning purity?

1. When I know, recognize, and accept myself as a soul, then I will be able to assimilate the quality of purity.
2. The intrinsic quality of the soul is purity. The original eternal form of I, the soul, is pure. Impurity is an external influence.

Purity serves as a fundamental virtue, laying the groundwork for attributes such as cleanliness, peace, and happiness. It is the nurturing force that gives birth to happiness and peace. Pure souls are inherently joyful, free from sorrow, anxiety, and restlessness. Adopting an attitude of universal brotherhood towards everyone is one way to foster purity.

This degree of purity functions as a source of power, enabling the accomplishment of much through pure thoughts alone. The power of purity can transform any individual's vision, attitude, and actions. Purity is closely connected to reality.

BLISS: A JOY BEYOND THE SENSES

Bliss is a supreme happiness, a profound joy that the soul experiences. True spiritual bliss is a feeling that involves our complete being. Bliss is not just a physical sensation without understanding. Your intelligence, mind, attitude, and everything is involved in this unified feeling of joy beyond the senses. You cannot get this joy from the physical world of sensory perception.

I want to share one experience of bliss I had recently. I was dancing without my body moving. The feeling was that the soul was dancing and singing, and the whole world came alive. While this was happening, I was sitting down in meditation! Everything was poetic, and I felt I was dancing without any of my limbs moving. The sound of the leaves, the trees, and the sky was alive. There was music in my mind, the soul was just dancing, and all I did was just be my original true self.

Bliss is our natural state of well-being and joy when we let go of all negativity in our minds. It is not a joy we experience because a situation happened. The soul feels this aliveness and joy every single moment because it is coming from so deep inside. Everything around you brings you joy because of what you feel inside. The world becomes like music.

Sometimes, bliss comes from seeing and hearing profound spiritual truths. There is a simple formula I use for experiencing bliss. I noticed that when my consciousness reflects on eternal truths, it is blissful. Think about it: if your consciousness reflects on transgressions that have happened to you, you automatically feel sorrow. When you are completely in the now and connected to eternal truths, then you experience bliss.

KNOWLEDGE: THE ENDLESS QUEST FOR TRUTH

We're discussing spiritual knowledge, which represents true awareness and understanding of reality, as opposed to perceptions or feelings based on illusion. The soul is eternal, knowledgeable, and blissful—three fundamental aspects of consciousness. Knowledge is an intrinsic quality of the soul, and through knowing, we realize and express our true selves.

When the soul experiences true knowledge, it remains aware of the vastness of the unknown. The soul never believes it has learned everything; instead, it maintains a learner's attitude. This recognition of the universe's expansive knowledge and endless secrets inspires a continuous desire to learn and understand more.

To allow the soul to flourish with spiritual knowledge, one must engage in contemplation and embrace silence while pondering eternal questions. Pose an eternal question to yourself, such as "Who am I?" and sit in silence, patiently waiting for the answer to surface. Each time you practice this, you will encounter a unique experience. There is merit in exploring silence and contemplating from a deeper space rather than solely relying on the analytical mind. Since the soul inherently possesses knowledge, silence merely opens the door, allowing that knowledge to rise and become consciously recognized.

Within our subconscious, all knowledge is recorded, revealing our original characteristics of wisdom, and understanding. This insight opens the third eye, and we become self-realized, experiencing ourselves as elevated beings, and recognizing our true identities as souls.

As our understanding expands, our happiness grows. Purity is the foundation of knowledge, while the proof of knowledge lies in feeling whole again. Humility is the hallmark of a knowledgeable person. Knowledge, like the sun, cannot remain concealed. Though some may deny the sun's existence during the night, no one can dispute the illuminating presence of the rising sun that brightens the day.

MEDITATION: REDISCOVERING INTRINSIC QUALITIES

* *Breathe in and out deeply while going deeper and deeper into your sacred center. Allow yourself to be, allow yourself to be in the moment. No need for any story. It is simple enough just to exist at this moment. Now, permit yourself to empty the contents of the world out of your mind, so that you can come home to the eternal you.*

* *As you settle in your home space, direct your focus inward. Concentrate your attention on the point in your forehead where you, the soul, reside. Continue to breathe in and out deeply and "see" yourself as a luminous being of light.*

* *Remind yourself: "I am Peace. This is my true essence. I am free from conflict. I, the soul, am serene and still. Within me, there is a deep sense of calm and contentment, undisturbed by thoughts and emotions."*

* *Take a moment now to visualize and reflect upon living in the light of peace. Envision this powerful light of peace emanating from within you.*

* *Contemplate how it would feel to express this pure peace in your relationships. How would it transform your connections and interactions with others?*

* *Next, consider the experience of infusing your daily actions with this profound sense of peace. How would it change the way you approach your tasks and responsibilities?*

> * *Take a few more moments and just be in your inherent quality of peace. You feel connected with your innate peaceful nature. You realize that each time you focus on peace and give it your attention, you are nurturing one of your most essential qualities. Embrace this peaceful energy and carry it with you throughout your day.*

In the meditation described above, the focus was on reconnecting with peace. However, you can personalize this meditation by incorporating any of the soul's primary qualities in place of peace. By doing so, you can explore and strengthen various aspects of you, the soul, deepening your understanding and connection to your true self. This versatile approach allows you to experience the full spectrum of the soul's original qualities, enriching your meditation practice over time.

For deep transformation and self-mastery, it is essential to concentrate on your original qualities daily. Treat your meditations on the primary qualities as a daily necessity, just like breathing and eating. Your soul's health relies on the oxygen of daily practice.

Access free meditations to go deeper into your quest for immortality:

These Soul Fitness meditations will pave the way for your true spiritual nature to unfold, illuminate, and spread joy to yourself and the world.

Go here to get access now:

shireenchada.com/soulfitness

15

MASTERING YOUR MIND

As I mentioned earlier, the soul is joined to the body. Our souls live in our bodies. We need the body to operate in this world, but we are not the body, just as the driver is not the car. When the soul contacts the brain, then it formulates thoughts. To think (aka mind), to analyze (aka intellect), and to hold experiences (aka impressions) are different aspects of our consciousness, much like different organs in the body.

In this chapter, we will explore the first aspect of consciousness -- the mind. Just as in physical fitness, one must train and focus on specific body parts to achieve results, we will explore the mind in this chapter. Subsequent chapters will be devoted to intellect and impressions, much like a fitness plan that includes different workout routines for various elements of the body.

The soul generates thoughts (it is important to remember - neither the body, the brain, nor the mind generates thoughts.) And these thoughts come up in the mind. So, the mind is the messenger of the soul. The mind can be compared to several things in the physical world. I'm going to give a couple of examples to make it clearer.

The mind is where thoughts arise. It is the computer screen of the soul. Visualize yourself sitting in front of a computer with a screen and keyboard. You bring up a file, and it appears on the screen. The soul works in much the same way. Just as the screen is not the computer, so the mind is not the soul. You, the soul, generate thoughts that appear on the "screen" of the mind. The mind is that part of our consciousness that enables us to visualize and create ideas. It is where all our experiences and desires arise.

Consciousness is often compared to an iceberg in that most of it is submerged beyond our sight, and only a part is visible. If we go with this analogy, we can say that 70 percent of our consciousness is submerged. The 30 percent that is above water is the mind.

The mind, like physical fitness, requires regular exercise and conditioning to reach its full potential. And this mind works with the energy of thought. So, where do thoughts come from? Yes, you are right, from the soul! The mind is one of the faculties of the soul. Just as we can't say, "I am my eyes or ears," but rather, "I have a set of eyes and ears." In the same way, we can say that the soul has a mind.

When the soul comes in contact with a body and enters the womb, the soul connects with the brain. From then on, the brain and soul operate together in the physical world. The brain is not the mind. The mind is metaphysical (beyond the physical), it is consciousness, and the brain is a complex physical object.

16

SCULPTING MENTAL MUSCLES: UNLOCKING THE MIND'S POTENTIAL

To chisel away stress and carve inner peace, we must first comprehend the origins of anxiety, stress, and sorrow. The common misconception is that our minds are solely responsible for these struggles. As discussed in the previous chapter, the mind is merely the soul's emissary, relaying messages about the soul's condition. Blaming the mind and attempting to forcefully control thoughts is akin to shooting the messenger.

Think of the mind as a canvas for thoughts, much like a computer screen displaying text and images. Even in sleep, our minds remain active. Thoughts are the life force of a soul, persisting until the body ceases to live. Emptying the mind of thoughts will neither bring peace nor is it feasible while the soul inhabits the body. To achieve mental tranquility, two essential steps must be taken:

1. Purify the mind by eliminating negative thoughts.

2. Nourish the mind with a consistent diet of wholesome thoughts rooted in timeless truths.

With these goals in mind, let's embark on our mental workout, sculpting our mental muscles to achieve balance and serenity.

Chiseling Away Stress: Carving Inner Peace

The secret to achieving peace of mind is to make our mind loving and to care for it spiritually at all times.

- Relax by watching your breath go in and out of your body. Watch how fluidly it moves in and out, in and out, in and out.
- Connect to that quiet place inside you, the still point of calm. You are a peaceful soul. Peace is your original innate quality. You need not seek peace outside. It is right within you. No one can give it to you or take it away from you. Only you hold the power to experience your intrinsic peace.
- Now, shower good wishes and pure feelings on yourself. Say to yourself, "I have the power to go beyond this physical dimension, this body, this role, this place and time – it is all but a speck of eternity."
- Now, shower your good wishes and pure feelings on all the people in your life that come to mind. "They have an identity beyond this physical dimension. They are also peaceful souls."

- Now come back to the awareness of you being an eternal soul and repeat to yourself, "All will be well. I am peace. All will be well. I am peace. All will be well. I am peace."

- To chisel away stress and carve inner peace is the greatest gift you can give yourself. And it is completely in your control to do so. The more deeply you reflect on peace, the more your mind is quieted. Affirm to yourself, "I will give my thoughts the right direction so that they bring me peace of mind."

CRADLING THE INNER CHILD: NURTURING YOUR MIND WITH LOVE

The mind is like a toddler. Just as a toddler would, your mind needs you to pay attention to it, be available, and give it care. Talk to your mind silently with love and encouragement balanced with firmness. Don't be harsh with it by scolding it. In this exercise, we will explore how to take care of our minds and give them nourishing food.

- Imagine yourself taking a walk outside on a still, clear moonlit night. There is a gentle breeze flowing. Take a moment to breathe in that stillness and become as quiet as the night.

- Now look at the full moon and absorb the light of the moon. You've become the light. You are a luminous eternal soul. You are love. Love for yourself is a deep memory embedded within you.

- Now ask yourself, "Do I feel any pain? Do I feel any anxiety?" Now imagine that a toddler under your care felt the same things. How would you respond to the child? Access that deep place of love and talk to yourself, "I am luminous eternal light. This feeling is temporary. Eternally, I am a peaceful soul. All will be well. This situation will pass. I am light. There is so much more to me than this feeling. I am eternally love and light."

Do this exercise at least once daily for a few weeks. Eventually, you will get into the habit of doing it while doing your daily chores.

Dismantling the Seven Deadly Cs: Loving the Mind

The seven deadly "Cs" are a group of negative behaviors and attitudes that can hold you back from living a joyful life. They are Comparison, Cynicism, Competitiveness, Controlling, Complaining, Criticizing, and Condemning. To help cleanse your mind and free yourself from these destructive habits, you can practice a simple yet powerful exercise. While we'll focus on one of the "Cs" as an example, remember that this exercise can be adapted to tackle any of the others. You just need to choose a word that's the complete opposite of the deadly "C" you want to break free from. For instance, let's focus on the deadly "C" of cynicism. The opposite of cynicism might be "trust."

- Sit in a quiet spot where you won't be disturbed for a few minutes. Take a few deep breaths, and while releasing those breaths, relax into yourself. For a minute or two, just meditate on your breath. Watch it move in and out of your body.

- Now, gently go inward and connect to that still point of consciousness within. Keep reminding yourself, "I am a pure soul. My original nature is to have a clean mind. I'm cleansing my mind." By pouring loving thoughts into your mind, you allow your mind to relax completely.

- One of the first ways to cleanse the mind of cynicism is to focus on the real self and on trust as the self's innate quality. Continue conversing with yourself, "At this moment, I give myself the gift of trust. I allow the energy of trust to wash away cynicism. It is so much better to see the world around me with innocent eyes. I accept that there is something good and beautiful within every human being and every situation. I choose to focus on that instead of thinking that nothing works for me. I give myself the gift of trust. I use my power to remain innocent. I trust."

- Commit to giving yourself this gift daily. Keep reminding yourself, "I trust. I trust. I trust. I trust things will work out for me. It's so easy to be free from cynicism."

Soul Foodie: Feeding Your Mind with Care

Intense care is given to how our food tastes, its nutritional value, and whether it is organic or non-GMO. We should put the same care into the "food" we put in our minds.

- Just for a few moments, allow your mind to completely relax. Permit yourself to enter that calm, quiet sanctuary of the mind. You are silent. You are still.

- Remember that your mind is but one aspect of your consciousness. It is the "computer screen" of the soul. Say to yourself, "I won't deny anything that appears on the screen of my mind." Lovingly witness your thoughts. Don't judge, scold, or suppress any thoughts. Keep reminding yourself, "These thoughts are messages from myself, the soul."

- Now, prepare to feed your mind. Gently nudge your mind toward healthy, eternal thoughts. Nourish your mind with thoughts such as, "I am a soul. I am consciousness operating this body. I am a transcendent being of light. I am peace. I am peace. I am a peaceful soul."

- Go back and forth between mindfulness of your thoughts, observing your thoughts, and gently feeding your mind eternal concepts.

Soul Reprieve: Embracing Moments of Rest

Just like we need good rest for physical well-being, in the same way, on a soul level, we need spaces of deep rest. This is not something good to have or one of our many wants; it is a basic need of the soul. We need to rest from our story, from our thoughts, from situations for small moments, and give our chaotic thoughts a break.

- Take a few slow deep breaths. Allow the breath to move fluidly in and out.

- Visualize yourself entering a room. In the room, there is a big table. Now, visualize taking your story and leaving it on the table. Do this one by one, to your beliefs, your situations, and even your thoughts. Take your time and slowly shed them all.

- And prepare now to leave the room. Turn your back on them at this moment. Now, you are entering a space of total silence. A beautiful sanctuary of light. In this space, you can feel your innocence. It is like nothing has ever happened to you. You are connected to the eternal you. Your mind is carefree and quiet. Take your time and savor this restful space of being beyond all stories untouched by the world. You are in a sanctuary of restful silence.

- Ask yourself the question, "If nothing had ever happened to me, who would I be?" Take your time and let the answer come to you. Feel that sense of freedom and innocence that comes from stepping away from your story. Permit yourself to ask yourself this question periodically. Allow yourself to take a break from your story and enjoy the feeling of being refreshed.

Echoes of Compassion: Radiating Love to the World

Dadi Janki (1916 to 2020), a prominent spiritual figure from India who led the Brahma Kumaris (recognized as the largest global spiritual organization managed by women), once said to me, "If you take care of other people's sorrow, then God will take care of your sorrow." To this day, this is one of the main tenets that I live by.

When I think of compassion, the image that comes to me is the Buddhist Goddess of Compassion, Kuan Yin. Interestingly, it means, "observing the sounds (or cries) of the world." Compassion is our ability to respond to the sound of sorrow in the world, as a mother would to a crying child. To truly respond to the cries of distress in the world, we need a silent mind, a mind that is free from selfish desires and our own story.

- Take a moment now and visualize yourself sitting by a still mountain lake. It is absolutely silent here. Breathe in this stillness and breathe out any stress and worry. Do this a few times till the silence infuses every part of your being. You feel completely relaxed.

- Now prepare yourself to plant this silence in the world through your mind. Visualize yourself sitting high up in the world on a cloud of light. Fill your mind with light and love. Now pour this light and love and imagine it cascading like a waterfall down on the world below. Feel this compassion and light as it pours through you onto the world. Imagine it washing away the worries of the world and bringing solace to every mind.

- Breathe in this compassionate light again and again and again and pour it onto the world. You begin to realize that as it refreshes the world, it soothes your mind. You are the first beneficiary of this love and light.

- Affirm to yourself, "I have to send out peaceful love and light to the world around me." You can do this while doing other things, while you are in a meeting, or around people. It is so easy to send the world pure energy of compassion. This practice will perform wonders in your life.

Access free meditations to go deeper into your quest for immortality:

These Soul Fitness meditations will pave the way for your true spiritual nature to unfold, illuminate, and spread joy to yourself and the world.

Go here to get access now:

shireenchada.com/soulfitness

17

AWAKENING THE INNER BUDDHA: CULTIVATING YOUR DISCERNMENT

In this chapter, we will explore the second aspect of consciousness, *buddhi* or intellect or intelligence, which is even subtler than the mind. The Sanskrit word *buddhi* indicates our deep rational power and is derived from the same root as the word Buddha, "one who is awake and wise." *Buddhi* also means wisdom, discernment, good judgment, right awareness, and right understanding. A sharp *buddhi* / intellect quickly and clearly distinguishes truth from falsehood, real from counterfeit.

The intellect makes proper distinctions. What is right or wrong? What should we do or not do? What is spirit, and what is matter? *Buddhi* makes these crucial distinctions. This intellect helps the soul to understand and reason properly. We all possess an intellect. For some, it is smart and focused; for others, it is dull and neglected.

Let's take any competitive sport. To win, an athlete must be in shape but also needs both intelligence and technique. In much the same way, we need intelligence and technique to be in total

Soul Fitness. Similarly, when we work out at the gym, we must understand which exercises to do, how many repetitions, how many times a week, etc. This requires intelligence. To be fit, we must be smart. In the same way, Soul Fitness requires a smart and focused intellect. We must be wise, discerning, and fully awake.

If you think about it, intellect is the key faculty of human consciousness. When we strengthen our intellect, it guides us through life. Only a smart, discerning intellect can find solutions to questions such as: How do I get my soul in shape? How do I stay in shape? How do I apply Soul Fitness in life? Intelligence tells us how to engage the right spiritual techniques at the right time.

Harnessing the Power of the Intellect for Mental Clarity

For the intellect to effectively perform its role, it requires spiritual wisdom and silence. With these two elements, the intellect can perceive all the components of the whole, recognize their differences, and make informed decisions. While it may sound simple, the intellect has to undertake numerous tasks, including:

- Filtering our thoughts: The practice of yoga can serve as an analogy for this process, as it emphasizes cultivating mindfulness, concentration, and inner peace. Through various postures, breathing exercises, and meditation, yoga practitioners learn to quiet their minds, filter out distractions and disruptive thoughts, and create a harmonious mental environment. This mirrors how our intellect filters out clamorous thoughts and promotes peace and harmony within ourselves.

- Navigating our inner world: Interval training serves as an apt illustration of this process. In interval training, participants alternate between high-intensity exercise and periods of rest or lower-intensity exercise, showcasing the ability to switch between different levels of intensity. Similarly, our intellect helps us "mute" the cacophony of our minds, such as cynicism and control issues, while allowing us to focus on the quieter, more harmonious thoughts, and aspects of ourselves. Just as interval training necessitates concentration and discipline to transition between varying exercise intensities, using our intellect to navigate our inner world calls for focus and self-awareness.

- Emphasizing spiritual growth: The role of a personal trainer can be compared to the intellect's ability to help us navigate the world's challenges while focusing on our spiritual growth. Just as a personal trainer offers guidance, expertise, and support to assist clients in achieving their fitness goals without becoming overwhelmed by external factors, the intellect enables us to uphold our commitments to the world without being disturbed by it. In this way, we learn to care for the happiness of others and the world around us, concentrating on our spiritual practice and seeking solutions that resonate with our spiritual values.

We benefit from a strengthened intellect as it:

- guides us to our real life as eternal souls.
- inspires us to find joy beyond the physical senses.
- inspires us to see reality.

- brings clarity.
- rejuvenates and recharges us.
- learns and relearns and so helps us make the right choices.

We will reactivate our original *Buddhi*, our reason, awareness, and understanding, by doing the exercises in the next chapter and performing actions in soul awareness.

18

STRENGTH TRAINING THE SOUL: EXERCISING THE INTELLECT

Fitness experts say that for strength training, we must eat right and lift heavy. This is also true for strength training the soul. We feed our intellects nourishing thoughts filled with eternal truths. And the lifting heavy is focusing our intellect on the exercises in this chapter. The longer the intellect is concentrated on these exercises the stronger it will become. Concentration is the operative word here. We have to minimize distracting thoughts while doing the exercises. I will outline how to do this as we go through the exercises.

Importantly, the intellect spiritually awakens the soul. We are so focused on the physical world and our mundane lives that we don't notice how our soul has gone to sleep. So now, raise your right hand and promise yourself and me that you will stay awake spiritually for at least a few minutes each day. This chapter's exercises are designed to keep us awake for that time. This helps the intellect to wake up fully and function spiritually.

To make sure we understand each other, let's explain two words. We'll use "step" to mean a thought, like "I am a soul" is one "step." Every exercise in this chapter has four "steps." When we put four "steps" together in the right order for each exercise, let's call it a "routine." We should follow the "steps" in order when doing the exercises. For optimal strengthening of the intellect (based on my personal experience), we need to do eight "routines" of exercise each day.

LEARNING TO TRUST YOURSELF TO MAKE THE RIGHT CHOICES

I've experienced that soul consciousness reveals the truth about everything. It is like the rising sun that shines light on everything. Also, we must be careful to make choices from our soul space instead of from a space of discontent. We should never make choices to run away from something, but because we are going toward something higher. Finally, remember to follow your conscience, and your path will reveal itself to you.

1. Become aware of yourself, "I am a soul. I express myself through the vehicle of this body. I'm a spiritual being. This is the real me."

2. Let conscience guide your life. Fill your intellect, your awareness, and understanding with thoughts that deserve to see the light of day. Fill your intellect with simple thoughts of self-knowledge and humility.

3. Now, clearly see the difference between temporary and eternal things. Become aware of the material world and see how temporary it is. It begins and ends. Notice how our time here is but a speck of eternity. Remind yourself, "I, the soul, am eternal. Deep inside, I can make the right choices."

4. Trust. Trust that the universe will actually reveal the choice to you. Don't force a decision. Trust cosmic timing. The path will become clear when it is supposed to become clear.

Taking Courageous Steps: Cultivating Willpower

Willpower tries to choose what is real and true. It acts well when it seizes the moment when it is present in the now, and does something powerful in this very moment. You must become very still and block out all the other voices in your head to achieve this. To cultivate this deep stillness and steely determination, one must make sincere spiritual efforts. Waste thoughts create a brick wall that blocks our efforts. Here are some typical waste thoughts: "I'll do it later." "These things will never stop." "Other people are fine without doing it." "My health doesn't permit it."

"Others aren't in my situation; that is why they can do it." With one determined thought you can leap over this wall. What is that powerful thought? "I must be the one who does this." Transform all the plans in your head to, "I will do it. And I will do it now." Don't listen to others. Don't look at others. Stay focused and jump over all your obstacles with this thought, 'If I take one step of courage, I will receive a thousandfold help." Let's start our steps:

1. Focus your intellect on this thought: "I am a luminous, pulsating spiritual star. For this moment, there is only I, the soul." Block out all distractions by staying focused for a few seconds.

2. Allow yourself to transcend the physical world. You are light. You feel light. You don't feel the burden or heaviness of matter or situations. You feel double light. "I'm floating and rising, going higher and higher, I've come into a field of light."

3. Imagine yourself in a spiritual realm of light of absolute beauty and power. All your thoughts become reality here. From this spiritual field of light, and in this moment, invite support and power. Absorb this energy into yourself.

4. Remember that you only have the present. Future and past do not exist here. There is only this moment. Use this moment wisely and say to yourself, "I am the one who will do it. I will do it. I must do it. I will do it now."

JOURNEY TO CONVICTION

Faith starts with a decision. The intellect makes that decision. When the intellect is presented with spiritual concepts, it decides whether to accept them or not. Once the intellect accepts a spiritual concept, it needs to have the experience to keep sticking to that decision. When we have enough experiences of our true spiritual identity, then those decisions become convictions. Deep spiritual experiences depend on the following:

1. The length of time we can reflect on a spiritual concept without thoughts from the external world.
2. Keeping the monkey mind in tow; otherwise it will distract the intellect.

To tame the monkey mind, the intellect needs a series of 'steps' to reflect on. Initially, it is almost impossible for us to reflect on any one 'step' for too long. We have to give the intellect a set of steps so it can move around but under our guidance. Keep going from one step to the next with acceptance and understanding.

> 1. With understanding and visualization, remember, "I am a soul."
> 2. Without external distractions remember, "I am immortal. I am neither born nor will I die. I always exist."
> 3. "My original nature is divine."
> 4. "I will always be. This is who I am. I am light energy. I am immortal."

Breaking the Illusion: Unmasking Fear

Motivational speakers usually say that fear is nothing but false evidence appearing real. This is so true because fear casts an illusion, telling us that something we have will end. It makes us believe that when our relationships end, our source of money ends, our security ends, our peace will end, or even our life will end. To really see through this false evidence we have to go deep within, away from the physical world of form and time, and grasp the truth about ourselves.

1. Breathe deeply in and out and move into your center. Take another deep breath and allow yourself to go deeper into that quiet center. Take another deep breath and go deeper and deeper into your center. Now imagine that deep inside you is a switch that turns off all the chatter and noise of the mind. Turn this switch off now and relax into deep stillness.

2. Acknowledge the age of your body and go beyond it by remembering that you are light; you are living light that even death cannot finish. You are eternal. You are a timeless, ancient being moving through time and space with the help of that body. Keep reflecting, "The body has a life span, but I, the soul, will always be. I, the soul, have no beginning, no end." This type of self-reflection replaces the habit of fear.

3. Now take a few moments and remember, "I am a living light, and before I entered this world, this body, I was complete. I was complete with peace and was totally innocent. Deep within me, the soul is a mountain of love, peace, and joy." No matter what happens in the external world, when you practice being an eternal soul, these qualities will never leave you. No external situation or person can take them away from you. All you have to do is practice, "I am light, I am peace, I am love, I am joy." The more you practice, the more you will realize that you are pure, you are peace, and you are light. The more you realize this, the easier it will be to dispel the illusion of fear.

4. Now take a deep breath and remember again, "I, the soul, will always be. I, the soul, have no beginning, no end. I am light; I am peace; I am love; I am joy. And, most importantly, I am beyond endings. The most important things in my life have no expiration date. Because regardless of whatever happens, I am always light, I am always peace, and I am deeply loved."

Embracing Reality: The Art of Letting Go

Letting go and reality are deeply connected. To have a clear understanding of reality, we need to realize and let go of the following:

1. Let go of just seeing the physical world of form, touch, and measurements and see beyond the surface to the deeply spiritual nature of life and people. In this realm we are all connected, you and I; we belong to each other.

2. Let go of the noise in your head. Let go of the voices of doubt, insecurity, competitiveness, and criticism and step into a deep space of silence. This silence cleanses the mind of illusions.

3. Let go of being stuck in just this short time. You and I, we are eternal. Time is eternal. This time is but a speck of eternity. Look at the grand sweep of history and enjoy the magnitude and comfort of being eternal.

4. Let go of seeing just the sky and the stars and see beyond. See far, far beyond time and space into our spiritual Home where you and I live as eternal souls with our eternal Parent.

Let's see reality together:

> 1. Let go of the world of drama, your roles, your responsibilities, and other distractions, and stabilize yourself in your original real self. You are a soul that is immortal, imperishable, and immortal. Just savor this feeling of being immortal.

2. You are in a room of light. In this room, your mind is clean, clean of wasteful and negative thinking. It is totally quiet in this room. Allow yourself to enter this space of pure, restful silence. Be in this space for a few moments

3. Just be. Just be in the now. There is nothing to worry about or plan. This moment is spiritual; this moment is peaceful. You can touch the present moment with your thoughts. Embrace this second and make it beautiful.

4. Go beyond the sky and the stars and allow yourself to enter a space where there is only light. For miles and miles and miles, there is nothing but light. All you see in this realm of light are other living lights, souls, floating in this infinite expanse of light. Up above is your Parent. All of us are connected here. Absorb the absolute stillness of this realm. Once you have taken your fill, gently, like a bird, glide back down to your body. Take your time and witness the life around you. Now, you can see reality. You can see the natural order of life, the real nature of everything.

Illuminating and Purifying the "I"

This is one of the most important aspects of strength training of the soul. Our intellects misrepresent the word "I." When we say "I," this "I" is polluted with body consciousness. That is, we either think of the body or the labels of the body when we say "I." We have to make the "I" soul conscious. Whenever we say "I," we remember our true form of soul, of being light. The efficacy of the other exercises hinges on how well we perform this one. So, let's start.

1. Come into the awareness of being a soul. Silently with conviction, say to yourself, "I am a soul. I am light. See yourself as a tiny star behind your eyes in the center of your forehead.

2. Either aloud or silently, say "I."

3. As soon as you say the word "I," pull back within yourself and remember "I" means soul. Become aware, "I'm not this body. I am light."

4. Now, use "I" in a sentence while being aware of yourself as a soul. Not that body, not that gender, not that race, not any of the labels, but an eternal soul.

The Power of Concentration in Finding Silence

Silence is only a thought away. Silence is not an absence of thoughts, but it is about creating pure elevated thoughts, thoughts that bring the mind and intellect into harmony and deep rest. I go into the depth and breadth of experiencing deep silence in my meditation album, *The Sweet Melody of Silence*. For this chapter, I will outline one exercise from that album that is essential to experience silence – Concentration.

Concentration helps us transcend silence. We can concentrate on the power of pure thoughts. Hence, I always keep stock of what I call my "go-to pure thoughts." Whenever I'm faced with a disturbing situation or start to obsess over questions such as, "Why did it happen?" "How can I do this?" "What is going to happen next?" Or even when I over-analyze a situation or person, then I go to my stock of "go-to pure thoughts" and focus on them by looping them in my mind.

Make this exercise personal by picking four pure thoughts that speak to you. Take a moment to establish yourself in your set of pure thoughts. Remember they have to be pure, eternal thoughts. Then keep looping them in your mind without giving in to any external thoughts throughout the whole of the set. For example, if you have an outside thought (what am I eating for dinner), then make a mental note of it, and next time be firm with yourself and go through the set without any external thoughts. Use visualization and understanding to build your experience. The following are some of my go-to pure thoughts.

1. I'm a pure soul.
2. I'm a child of God.
3. As God's child, I have the same spiritual DNA as the Source. I have the same spiritual features and nature as the One.
4. God is the ocean of peace and love, and I'm a junior ocean of peace and love.

19

SPIRITUAL MUSCLE MEMORY: AWAKENING THE SOUL'S ORIGINAL QUALITIES

When you teach your body to ride a bike or play the clarinet, you actually create in your body a long-term memory of this motion, called muscle memory. Your body creates a physiological blueprint so that even if you take time off from the task, you return to it faster and easier than when you first learned how to perform it. Athletes and musicians have taken advantage of muscle memory for millennia.

This sub-section will discuss how to tap into your spiritual muscle memory and enjoy lifelong benefits. First, let's talk about the third aspect of consciousness called impressions, expressed by the Sanskrit word *sanskars*. This Sanskrit word expresses much more than mere impressions, and no one English word conveys the depth of *sanskars*.

Our actions leave impressions on the brain and soul. A lot of science explains how actions affect the brain, and so are habit forming, but here, we will talk about the imprints on the soul. Our actions and experiences leave imprints on the soul, resulting in internal after-effects. These legacy impressions are our belief systems, attitudes, habits, inclinations, and propensities. These impressions are stored as thoughts, thought patterns, memories, feelings, sounds, and images, and all of these together form our *sanskaras*, determining our individual uniqueness.

Understanding this third aspect of consciousness (*sanskars*) will help us not only manage our personal Soul Fitness regimen but also create individualized spiritual muscle memory. Our individual *sanskars* profoundly influence us. For example, if one is abused as a child, that *sanskar* still affects one today.

There are three kinds of *sanskars*:

- Negative
- Necessary
- Original

Negative *sanskars* include anger, fear, greed, laziness, insecurity, revenge, self-doubt, and a sense of inferiority to name a few. These negative *sanskars* create hopelessness and sorrow.

Necessary or essential *sanskars* involve learning practical skills, such as driving, playing a musical instrument, or cooking. Some of these *sanskars* have accumulated over many lifetimes.

The soul's original *sanskars* include love, peace, bliss, purity, and wisdom. These are the original qualities of the self -- this is where we all began before our original *sanskars* mixed with negative ones.

Fortunately, our negative *sanskars* are not eternal though now they definitely afflict the soul. We can regenerate and reclaim our original *sanskars* by relearning our spiritual muscle memories.

Just as we build muscle memory when we learn something new, whether it's how to snowboard or play the violin. Our brain fires up all the right muscle fibers to help us perform well. Once the brain tells your muscle fibers to move, they send feedback to your central nervous system, telling where your body is in space, so it knows what muscles to fire next. It's a continuous feedback loop between your brain and muscles. Movement becomes automatic as your brain creates pathways through your central nervous system. The more you use these pathways, the more your muscle memory solidifies, even if you slack off for a while, says Wayne Westcott, Ph.D., a fitness researcher.

Not surprisingly, building spiritual muscle memory is analogous to building physical muscle memory. Doing one or more exercises in this book triggers positive changes to your *sanskars* and awakens your deepest, dormant soul's original *sanskars*. These then start to play out in your life in very positive ways. The more exercises you do, the quicker you awaken your deepest, dormant soul's original *sanskars*. The more exercises, the purer the *sanskars* you deposit in your spiritual savings account. And as with any savings account, starting early is best – like right now! The game changer here is that you begin to build spiritual equity.

BUILDING SPIRITUAL EQUITY: AWAKENING THE BLISSFUL YOU THROUGH FOCUS MEDITATION

* *Begin by imagining yourself taking a dip in a clear, blue pristine lake of light. The surroundings are incredibly peaceful. You feel the cool waters of serenity as you take a dip, relaxing into yourself. With each subsequent dip, you let your stresses wash away and let go of all the situations in the world.*

* *Now ask yourself, "Who is the real me? What will I achieve when I focus on the real me?" Visualize yourself with a totally focused mind.*

* *Take your time and get a clear vision of the real you, the luminous you filled with love and joy. Allow yourself to see this version of yourself fully.*

* *Remind yourself daily, "To truly awaken the real me, I need determination and focus." Don't dwell on your shortcomings. Concentrate on the love, light, and wisdom deep inside of you. Your focus increases as you consistently remember the vision of the real you.*

Remember your deep consciousness never forgets, and by beginning even this one exercise, you can reasonably expect your innate *sanskars* to quickly regenerate, lasting for decades or even a lifetime.

20

CONSCIOUSNESS TRIAD: EXPLORING THE MIND, INTELLECT, AND *SANSKARS*

The mind, intellect, and *sanskars* – mentioned in chapters 15, 17, and 19 -- constitute our three primary states of consciousness. Just as the primary colors make up the whole color spectrum, so these three states of consciousness combine to form our entire spectrum of conscious states. Our thought processes, our decision-making, our clarity, and our love – all arise from these three cognitive components.

Let's do a quick recap:

- Mind is the soul's messenger. It tells us what is going on within the soul, and also it is the "screen" of the soul where thoughts are displayed.

- Intellect or intelligence is the rational, discerning part of the soul. Intellect gradually develops as we mature in life.

- *Sanskars* are our conscious and subconscious memories, experiences, attitudes, and belief systems.

Understanding the Mind, Intellect, and *Sanskars* Loop for Deep Transformation

It is essential to understand how all these cognitive faculties operate. By doing so, we can activate important parts of our consciousness that are now dormant. In this way, we realize our full potential.

I want you to visualize the mind, intellect, and *sanskars* as a loop, as shown in the diagram. Let's say, I like strawberries. The fondness began when my mom fed me one at age two. The strawberry's image, color, texture, and smell are imprinted on the soul, forming a *sanskar*. Both the soul and the brain carry this memory.

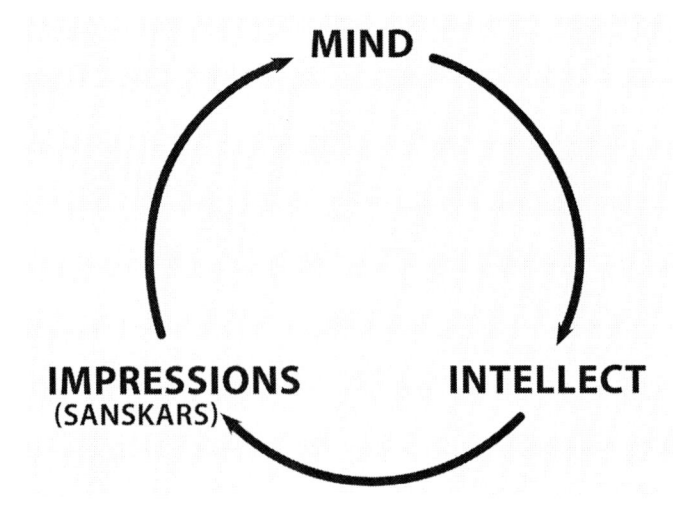

MIND → INTELLECT → IMPRESSIONS (SANSKARS) → MIND

Diagram A
Due to my positive initial experience, I'm drawn to strawberries and each time I eat them, my consciousness reinforces this preference. Over time, I crave them as this impression resurfaces in my mind.

This analytical model can be applied to understand addictions1, such as alcohol addiction. Imagine being a 16-year-old at a party where everyone, despite being underage, is drinking. You face heavy peer pressure to drink, though your parents forbid it. Your intellect engages in an internal debate: "Should I do it? What if I get caught?"

Suppose you give in to peer pressure, thinking it's a one-time thing. The experience—taste, smell, feelings—becomes imprinted on your *sanskar*. You feel more at ease and socialize after drinking thus forming a favorable impression. A few months later, at another party, you face the same pressure. This time, the debate is shorter (if it was 30 minutes the first time, it will be 15 minutes now) because you created a favorable impression and you drink again. The *sanskar* strengthens with each repetition, making drinking a habit.

As the habit strengthens, the intellect weakens, and the internal debate shortens to zero minutes over time. After years of this pattern, you reach a point where you crave alcohol without external influence. There's no debate, as the intellect is bypassed by a *sanskar* mind loop, forming a strong habit or addiction.

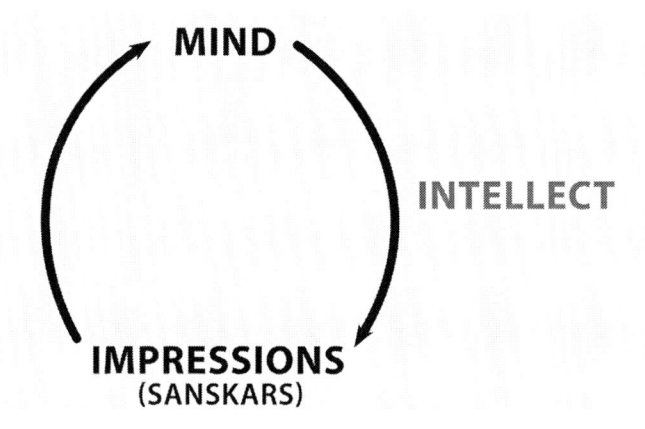

MIND

INTELLECT

IMPRESSIONS
(SANSKARS)

Diagram B
We live in this unhealthy loop of habitual or compulsive behavior for about 80% to 90% of our lives. We have so suppressed the intellect that it ceases to function. We live the majority of our lives without truly or deeply reasoning, without awareness. Our negative *sanskars* take control.

Let's examine Diagram A, focusing on the clockwise flow of thoughts/consciousness. The mind receives input from external sources through the senses or from *sanskars*. The soul's strength relies on the intellect's power; a robust, positive intellect empowers the soul, while a weak one diminishes it.

Sanskars can manifest as self-destructive thought patterns, such as compulsive feelings of inferiority, narcissism, loss of trust, or unhealthy dependencies. These thought patterns form our psychological reality, and to some extent, we all experience psychological addictions. Forcefully trying to break free from addictions is ineffective. Instead, fostering understanding and awareness is essential. By seeking intelligent, genuine alternatives, we can transform our minds and intellect's functioning. Otherwise, negative habits persist, leading to blame, shame, or regret.

Soul Fitness guides you through a natural process of transformation. Rather than battling negativity, we focus on reactivating our original, pure consciousness, our positive *sanskars*. To fully harness the benefits of Soul Fitness, we must connect our mind and intellect to our original *sanskars* through daily practice. Each day, we journey within to experience our innate pure qualities of peace and love. This process requires determination and the conviction that our true selves are composed of pure, sublime, and joyful qualities.

A Simple Test to Awaken Pure *Sanskars*

There are both negative and pure sanskars within each of us. Pure *sanskars* lead to a good life. Awaken them! To do this, we must strengthen our intellect by understanding and awareness. We strengthen our intellect by steadily remembering timeless truths about the soul. I want you to test this for yourself and see if your intellect really strengthens. Take this simple but powerful awareness, "I am a soul. I am light. I am timeless," and fix it in your mind. Now, take a few moments and understand this awareness fully. To make this work, you must also step away from all material concepts of yourself. Fill your mind with the simple understanding that "I am a soul." We experience the true beauty, magic, and power of Soul Fitness when we also put aside physical distractions.

Engaging the Triad: From Decision to Conviction Exercise

Faith begins with a choice made by the intellect. When confronted with spiritual ideas, the intellect decides whether to embrace or reject them. Once a spiritual concept is accepted, an experience is necessary to reinforce that decision. As we accumulate experiences affirming our spiritual essence, these decisions solidify our convictions.

Reactivating our innate divinity relies on two factors:

1. The ability to contemplate a spiritual concept for an extended period without external thoughts intruding.

2. Controlling the wandering mind to prevent distractions to the intellect.

To discipline the wandering mind, the intellect requires a sequence of 'steps' to contemplate. At first, maintaining focus on a single 'step' for an extended time might be challenging. Providing the intellect with multiple steps allows it to shift between them under our direction.

1. Comprehend and visualize the idea, "I am a soul."
2. Undisturbed by external distractions, remember, "I am eternal. I am not born, nor will I die. I always exist."
3. "My inherent nature is divine." Progress from one step to another with acceptance and understanding.
4. "I am everlasting. This is my true self. I am luminous energy. I am eternal."

In the above exercise, we are using all three faculties of the soul. Comprehension is part of the intellect, remembrance is the job of the mind, and divinity is within our *sanskars*. Through daily practice of the above exercise, we will be able to activate peace, love, and sublime joy within the soul.

Note: Addictions are complex, involving numerous factors beyond repeated consumption. While some individuals may abuse alcohol for years without addiction, others can become hooked from their first drink. Genetics plays a significant role in determining susceptibility to addiction. This example is simply to illustrate the mind-*sanskar* loop.

21

HEALING THE SPIRITUAL HEART: EMBRACING LOVE, COMPASSION, AND CONNECTION

In this context, when we discuss the heart, we are not referring to the physical organ within the human body. Instead, we mean the human capacity for love, compassion, and affection. As defined by Dictionary.com, the heart represents: 1. The innermost or central part of anything (in our case, consciousness), and 2. The center of emotion, particularly when contrasted with the head as the center of intellect.

For millennia, all over the world, people have talked about their heart as the center of their being, the center of their feelings and consciousness. There is a reason for this. People all over the world, throughout history, say the sky is blue because it is! In that spirit, as you do the exercises in this book, accept the spiritual heart as an important component of consciousness. This is the first step in healing our hearts. Often the physical heart seems okay but the spiritual heart needs healing.

Deep Self-Love: Healing the Spiritual Heart for Resilience

Nowadays, it's common to speak of loving the self. I agree, but this love has to be deep, not superficial. We must love ourselves with our hearts. It is not enough to intellectually accept ourselves as souls. We must truly love our original selves.

The heart is the center of our deepest awareness, and it is there we must find healing. If you do other exercises in this book but don't heal your heart, then it becomes a kind of intellectual game. We must awaken true self-love and self-respect.

At the risk of stating the obvious, healing our hearts is necessary for the following reasons:

- Sometimes, pain in the body can result from pain in the heart. To release pain in the physical body, the first step may be to heal the spiritual heart.

- When you release the pain in your heart, you increase your capacity to receive spiritual power.

- To live happily in today's world, you must strengthen your heart. This means strengthening our compassion and determination. Then no matter what happens sorrow will not overcome you.

- We achieve true Soul Fitness when our heart is clean and free of sorrow, confusion, and problems. Sorrow in the heart naturally weakens our wisdom.

Achieving Inner Harmony: The Connection Between Heart, Mind, and Intellect

1. Harmonizing heart and mind: The heart and mind are closely connected, and internal harmony between them allows healing to take place. Like a well-coordinated workout routine, when the mind and heart are completely aligned, we become fully integrated beings. This alignment fosters hope and a feeling of being capable of spreading happiness to the entire world. This book provides various exercises to heal your heart and align it with the mind.

2. Linking heart and vision: The heart and our vision of ourselves are intimately connected. This vision shapes our thoughts and firmly establishes itself within the heart. Much like visualizing our ultimate fitness goals, this vision of our totally spiritually fit self, originating from the heart, returns to the mind and influences our actions and progress. Seeing our final, completely soul-fit self is crucial in healing our hearts.

3. Connecting heart and intellect: The heart is also closely connected to the intellect. Like the strength gained from consistent exercise, the power of truth destroys the clutter in our hearts. When the intellect grasps eternal concepts and engages them, it remains steady, recognizing the value of truth.

4. Engaging in Soul Fitness: With understanding, we decide to truly engage in Soul Fitness and make a determined commitment to cleanse our hearts of ill will. This decision creates harmony among the mind, intellect, and heart, resulting in healing.

5. Realizing the impact of negative thoughts: The heart is where we realize that our negative thoughts cause us pain. Like acknowledging the need for a heart-healthy diet, when we have a deep feeling in our heart about something, we can engage the intellect, heal the heart, and strengthen the soul.

Cultivating a Joyful Heart for Emotional Well-Being

- Cultivating a happy heart leads to a refreshed mind. The state of your heart directly impacts your overall well-being, with a joyful heart contributing to a cool and clear mind.
- A pure heart fosters a sense of security. When your heart is clean, your mind follows suit, leading to feelings of safety and stability.
- The contents of your heart are reflected in your mind, highlighting the importance of maintaining a happy heart.
- By healing your heart, you become resilient to emotional pain and external negativity.
- Engaging your intellect to make a conscious decision to rid your heart of the ill will set the stage for healing and harnessing the power of a happy heart.

22

SOUL CARDIO: SIX TRANSFORMATIVE EXERCISES TO STRENGTHEN YOUR SPIRITUAL HEART

We need to look after our spiritual heart, as our soul craves it just like our body needs water. This is important because:

1. If you only focus on the other exercises in this book without nurturing your heart, it'll feel like a mind game without real meaning.
2. It doesn't matter how much money we have, the stuff we own, or how many people say we're amazing and attractive; if we don't truly feel good on the inside, we won't find real peace.

Inner emptiness will only grow if our heart isn't in the right place. I'm sharing six powerful exercises to help you care for your heart. To truly benefit from them, let these exercises touch your heart deeply.

KICKSTART YOUR DAY WITH PURE, LOVING FEELINGS

The first rule of a soul cardio workout is to avoid any bad feelings in the heart. Because your heart becomes what you think and feel. When we make our feelings for others pure, loving, and elevated, then we also absorb those feelings. We are the first recipients of all the pure feelings we give. So, let's begin our first exercise. It needs to be done at the start of each day.

- As soon as you wake up, start your day in quiet reflection and pour positive, loving thoughts into your heart. "I am a soul. I, the soul, am love. I am loving. I am lovable. I am loved."

- Now, give this love to everyone you see and think about. Don't hold back. The more you give, the more you will receive. Talk to yourself, "There is no limit to the love I give. I give. I give. I give."

- Be patient. Keep doing this every day for at least 2 to 3 weeks. You gradually clean out the dust of hurt and cynicism with a daily dose of loving thoughts such as these.

- Generating pure feelings either for the self or others means learning to create love inside your heart and silently giving it to everyone you meet. Keep doing this exercise every chance you get. Remember, only in giving is there receiving.

CULTIVATING SELF-LOVE

Self-love can be learned. It is a 'thought habit.' The first step and the last step of self-love is having deep regard for the self. You should see yourself with a vision of profound respect and care. This happens when you become aware of your true identity as a divine spiritual being.

- Gently but firmly let go of identifying yourself as just a mundane physical being. Go inside yourself and sense the soul that animates your body. Touch yourself, the soul, with your thoughts. Remember, "I am a soul. My original nature is love, peace, and divinity." Have regard for who you truly are.

- Talk to yourself as you would to a favorite child. Visualize a beautiful, innocent, precious child in front of you. What would you say to this child? Now say those same things to yourself. "I am precious. I am precious because of who I am, not because of what I possess or what I can provide externally." "I am innocent. I am sweet and lovely like a beautiful fragrant flower."

- Allow rays of care and peace to cascade all over the soul. Remember your true nature. Tell yourself, "I care about myself. I truly care about my original self – the real self. I am a deeply beautiful being beyond this material body."

- Keep seeing yourself with respect and care and notice how precious you truly are. Keep pouring thoughts filled with respect and love into your heart. When you do, you will experience them entering your heart. Sweetly converse with yourself at least 3-4 times a week.

Elevating Your Perspective: Overcome Disappointment and Empower Yourself

Sometimes we have a tendency to focus on everything that is not working or the weaknesses we can't seem to overcome. We are all disheartened at times. For me, disappointment is simply telling ourselves the wrong story. We need real wisdom to shift the story in our heads. For the next exercise to work, you must take a wise encouraging approach to yourself.

- Pick a situation or person that disheartens or demoralizes you. Take some time and go over all the reasons you feel this way. Give yourself space and time. Write out the reasons if you have to.
- Now, gently but firmly let go of the external world and become aware of yourself as a soul, a being of luminous energy. From this vantage point, you see yourself as an actor playing different roles, using the body as a costume. Tell yourself, "I am a soul. I, soul, am an actor playing different roles. This body is my costume. I travel through time. This role, this situation, is just one of my many acts."

- Now raise yourself about 30 feet above the situation and above your costume. Look down and see yourself as an actor on a stage and all the others around you as actors. Watch the situation as you would watch a play.

- Ask yourself, "Am I telling myself the right story about this situation or person? As a witness, what new perspective can I bring to it?" Don't insist that an answer come right away. Sometimes it takes days or even weeks for the right answer to emerge.

- Give yourself love and encouragement from up above. Keep watching the situation as a play. Have an encouraging conversation with yourself: "I am a soul. I am an actor. This act is challenging, but I can transform this situation and make it beneficial for everyone involved. Within me, there is a power that I have forgotten -- the power to transform my external environment with my pure thoughts. I can do this. I have mastery over the situation and over my mind, for I am a soul. I will not give up because this is actually easy for me to do."

- Repeat the steps till the story you tell yourself changes and becomes empowering instead of debilitating. If you repeat the exercise enough times, it will happen. You will feel encouraged and energized.

FINDING JOY IN YOUR OWN COMPANY

We are eternal souls. In our eternal journey through time we've had many costumes, played many different parts, and we've had many relationships with many actors. The only thing constant in this ever-changing cosmic play seems to be our own company! Relationships come and go, and people come and go, but I have to be with myself all the time. Hence, one of the greatest gifts we can give ourselves in life is the ability to enjoy our own company. For this exercise, let's create an inner meadow full of beautiful thoughts. Then everything we do will be a pleasure.

- Breathe in and out deeply a few times and relax. Prepare yourself to go on a spiritual picnic. Right now, leave the world of your to-do lists, meetings, and social media. Just let it go in this second. Leave that world behind and travel to a beautiful meadow inside. As you journey into this field of spirituality, notice how calm you feel. Notice how the air is fragrant with peace. There is a quiet joy here; you feel totally relaxed and blissful. This is your inner sanctuary.

- Allow yourself to lie here in this beautiful inner meadow and let the cool breeze of tranquility flow through you, soothing your mind. Blowing away the harsh feelings you have for yourself. Now, reflect on the values you care about most. You can see your innate goodness.

- Building on this, gently reveal to yourself, your caring and compassionate nature. On this inner picnic, you are feasting on your goodness, and you realize this innate nature is divine. You savor the feeling of being divine and pure.

- In this field of spirituality, your beauty is fully blossomed. You find a deep joy in being here with your true self. You feel fully awake and empowered. You love being with yourself. There is no moment like this moment and no company better than your own company. You feel full and joyful.

Soothing the Soul, Healing Your Heart

Endings such as death, breakups, or any loss can cause much pain. And, sometimes for no apparent reason, we feel deep sorrow in our hearts. In this exercise, we will gently calm down our chaotic thoughts and offer solace to our hearts. Let's begin:

- Take a few deep breaths and relax. This is a good time to switch off your phone and be still and by yourself. Now, imagine you, the soul, floating up toward the sky. You are going up and up and up. You arrive at a beautiful white soft cloud of white light.

- As you enter this cloud of light, you notice the serene coolness of this space. There is a soft white pillow in front of you, inviting you to lie on it. As you put your head on it, you feel the burden of pain and sorrow leaving you. You sink your head into this pillow while your heart sinks into silence. You let everything of the material world go and just be.

- You feel a gentle, beautiful, divine feather brushing your forehead. With each brush of the feather, you feel lighter and lighter and more and more comforted.

- Each brush of the feather makes you feel healed and loved. Just feel a loving, tender light pour into you. Now while still in this beautiful, serene cloud, imagine a healing, divine presence close to you. Imagine yourself deeply held by this divine light. Allow yourself to be comforted and connected by this light. Permit yourself to feel connected to all that is good and beautiful in the universe. Your head feels cool on this pillow, and your heart feels comforted. With each brush of the feather, you feel lighter and more connected.

- You return to the physical world knowing that this space filled with healing light is always available for you. It is just a few thoughts away.

The Art of Balanced Living: Mastering Love and Detachment

In spirituality, balance means most often balancing pairs of positives. It is never about doing something beneficial and not doing something beneficial but about doing two seemingly opposing beneficial acts in perfect balance and harmony. When you think of an old-fashioned scale, it needs something to be balanced on both sides for it to work properly. For your heart to be strong, for your mind to be focused, and for the soul to experience stillness, this inner scale needs to be fully balanced with being both loving and detached. On the scales of a good, healthy, balanced life, we need to balance detachment with love. Are you wondering why? Because:

1. When we are detached, then we can love from a pure place.

2. We experience real security. Not the kind where we need millions of dollars in the bank or a good home security system to feel secure but the real thing.

3. This sense of security will allow us to give without expectation. And, remember only in the giving is there receiving.

4. We will feel whole, nourished, and totally still.

Being equally loving and equally detached is one of the greatest living art forms. Even though this is not one of the easiest exercises to master, with practice and time, achieving that total stillness of a fully balanced scale is possible.

- To become detached, we need to master being a witness. Hence, simply observe the self. Observe your life as you would a movie. "I have a unique part to play in this grand epic movie called Life. I can't play someone else's part nor can anyone else play mine." Also, none of us play the same part each minute. It is a different scene every minute. What was there one minute ago is different the next moment.

- Now, take a few moments and go inside yourself and sense the spirit. The essence of who you are in that body, that costume. "I, the actor, dwell in the center of the forehead." Now, see yourself with a vision of love and respect. "I care about myself deeply. I'm absolutely precious and valuable. I'm a soul, I'm an actor, and I'm valuable to this play."

- Now prepare to observe a recent or distant scene of your life that caused you sorrow. Rewind the film in your mind's eye and watch it as you would watch an animated movie. When watching an animated movie and a character experiences a challenging situation, you are simultaneously aware of 1. It's just an animation so you don't get too invested. 2. If you rewind it to the beginning of the movie, the character's journey starts anew. So, now sit on the seat of a detached observer and just keep watching your scene as you would an animated film.

> - Now ask yourself the question, "Who would I be if nothing has ever happened to me? No bad scenes, no harshness, no loss, no pain? How would I feel?" Move into the feeling of being totally innocent. The soul, the actor, hasn't played any part yet. In this state, the soul is pure, the soul is trusting, and the soul is totally innocent. Now shower love to yourself in this state. "I love me. I'm a soul that is untouched by matter, untouched by events, and untouched by time. I am pure, sweet, and lovely."

Repeatedly doing this exercise helps you achieve inner harmony. By learning to be detached, you can balance pairs of positives, such as love and detachment. This balance allows us to experience pure love, real security, and a sense of wholeness and stillness.

**Access free meditations to go deeper
into your quest for immortality:**

These Soul Fitness meditations will pave the way for your true spiritual nature to unfold, illuminate, and spread joy to yourself and the world.

Go here to get access now:

shireenchada.com/soulfitness

23

MEMORY TRACK: THE BRIDGE BETWEEN CONSCIOUS AND SUBCONSCIOUS REALMS

You are feeling fine one moment and then all of a sudden, your mood is off. Do you experience that sometimes? Something is coming up and you are not sure what's wrong. All of that is because our psychological memory track is not clean.

Whenever I think of the memory track, I think of those old cassette tapes (I know, I'm dating myself here! For all those young ones who don't know what I'm talking about, look it up on the internet.) It's like we have a junked-up cassette tape inside with a lot of stuff recorded and then re-recorded on top of the old recording. At random times this junked-up cassette tape just keeps playing. When you want to play one song, in the middle it plays something else that was recorded before the song. This is because our memory track is not clean.

CLEARING THE SOUL'S MEMORY TRACK

The memory track represents the sum of everything retained by the conscious mind. Within the soul, we have a memory track, which is a collection of conscious and unconscious events and people. The memory track is that part of our consciousness from which we recollect specific experiences. Throughout our lives, many things have happened, but certain experiences leave a deeper imprint on our memory. Some events you might not even remember, but others leave a lasting mark on your memory track. What you recall from something that might have happened ten years ago is what remains on the surface of your memory track.

I see the memory track as a bridge between the conscious and subconscious mind. It can be accessed by both realms. When something appears before me and evokes feelings in response, the memory track is activated, and emotions come to the surface. The memory track serves as the connecting layer between the two realms of the mind.

The memory track is subtle. Just as *sanskars* are the record of my actions and interactions, the memory track is the impact of everything stored in my memory. This expresses itself in my nature, *sanskars*, and old memories. One moment we feel everything is going well, life couldn't be better, and then we see someone or hear something, and suddenly our mood changes. This memory track, containing our old nature and memories, brings emotions and thoughts to the surface.

Emotions connect the memory track and the conscious mind—they are memories stirred by something—latent things buried from the past that we may not even be aware of. Emotions can be either negative or positive. I find it interesting that the word "emotion" contains the word "motion." Emotions are conscious, instinctive mental reactions that move from the memory track to the conscious mind.

Negative emotions from the conscious mind push themselves onto the memory track because the memory track is not clean. If we don't cleanse the memory track of useless and negative emotions, feelings, and thoughts, we won't be able to perceive and experience the truth. This, in turn, prevents us from savoring bliss. To purify the memory track, we need to replace it with pure and elevated thoughts. We must build up our pure, eternal, spiritual thoughts so they wash away the other memories.

In my experience, adhering to a Soul Fitness regimen means we need to work with aspects that are within our control. To maintain a sustainable practice, we must first nourish our minds with pure and eternal thoughts. Doing so cleanses the memory track, which then begins to influence the subconscious mind, even though it's not always directly accessible to us.

Here are some additional reasons why we need to cleanse the memory track:

- To stop worrying: We often worry excessively because we cling to memories.
- To experience beauty: A cleansed memory track allows for more beautiful experiences.
- To embrace the truth: When truth subtly enters the memory track, falseness and illusions fade away.

- To concentrate our minds: The mind tends to wander when old memories keep resurfacing.
- To regain vitality: Old feelings and memories within the memory track can deplete our energy.

Soul Fitness is about engaging in sustainable exercises that we can practice independently. We don't want to feel disheartened by aspects of our psyche that we can't control. Since the memory track is the innermost layer we can work with, let's focus on cleansing it.

Memory Track Alchemy: Transforming Negativity Into Stillness

To embark on a journey of spiritual development, it's crucial to cleanse our memory track. By purifying this inner layer of our consciousness, we can eliminate negative thoughts and emotions, ultimately paving the way for a more joyful life. Here are some steps to help you cleanse your memory track:

1. Awareness, awareness, awareness: Develop attentiveness to your thoughts by integrating eternal concepts into your everyday life. When you notice a negative thought, deliberately substitute it with an eternal thought like, "I am a spiritual being having a human experience." Eternal truths aid in accessing and gently purifying your memory track, fostering a more profound connection with your true self.

2. Engage in spiritual study: Immerse yourself in a spiritual study that provides wisdom and insight. By absorbing pure

and eternal thoughts, you'll replace old, negative memories with enlightening ideas.

3. Surround yourself with positive influences: The people and environments we interact with can significantly impact our memory track. Seek out individuals who inspire and support your spiritual journey, and limit exposure to negative influences.

4. Adopt a compassionate diet: Our diet and mental well-being are intimately linked. Choose a vegetarian lifestyle, prioritizing a compassionate approach to nourishing your body. This conscious choice will contribute to cleansing your memory track and supporting your spiritual journey.

5. Consistency is key: Use the exercises provided in this book and commit to consistent practice. Set aside moments for stillness, immerse yourself in self-reflection, and approach the cleansing of your memory track with unwavering determination and devotion.

Following these steps and committing to a Soul Fitness regimen will gradually cleanse your memory track and create a strong foundation for spiritual growth, stillness, mental clarity, and inner harmony.

24

UNLOCKING INNER BLISS: THE BENEFITS OF AWAKENING YOUR CONSCIENCE

We all have done things in our lives that we are not proud of or regret. Things for which we can't seem to forgive ourselves. This regret is coming from our conscience. When we perform actions against the universal moral code, our conscience "bites" us. I like to use the word bite because it is almost like there is a sting to it. Conscience is the same for all human beings regardless of race, culture, nationality, or gender because there truly is a common overarching moral code. Just that for some this conscience is asleep, and for some it is awake. It is in our best interest to awaken our conscience on our terms when we can deal with it. Otherwise, there will come a time when we will be stuck up the creek without the proverbial paddle.

Why do we need to awaken our conscience?

- Strengthens inner listening: Awakening our conscience empowers us to listen to ourselves quietly and supports the internal work needed to reach our peaceful selves.

- Frees us from guilt: An awakened conscience allows us to break free from guilt, which can hold us back from improving our state of mind.
- Releases us from deception: When our conscience is awakened, we no longer feel deceived by others.
- Calms the inner voice: Awakening our conscience helps quiet the shrill inner voice, enabling us to lead a serene life.
- Achieves inner peace: To experience true peace, our conscience must be quiet. Understanding and awakening our conscience is essential for this process.

Conscience: The Soul's Compass

Conscience is an inner sense of right and wrong that guides our conduct. It encompasses the complex ethical and moral principles that govern our actions and thoughts. Our conscience is aware of what is right and wrong, and it differentiates between truth and falsehood. If we were to relate it to the primary aspects of consciousness discussed in previous chapters, conscience would be an aspect of the *buddhi*, or intellect.

All human beings possess a conscience, which is incredibly subtle. It helps us clearly distinguish between right and wrong. It may seem as though some people, including certain political leaders, lack a conscience. However, everyone has a conscience. The issue arises when, despite the conscience signaling that something is not right, the mind suppresses it. Over time, this suppression can cause the conscience to go dormant.

When does the conscience become dormant?

- Under the sway of friends, family, and social groups, whether in-person or online
- Emphasizing materialism excessively
- Engaging in destructive behaviors repeatedly
- Clutching onto past issues
- Harboring numerous useless and negative thoughts
- Squandering excessive amounts of time

LESSONS FROM DADI JANKI'S UNWAVERING SPIRIT

During my time spent with Dadi Janki, I understood the true meaning of conscience. To her, it wasn't about grand gestures or dramatic decisions but about consistently choosing to do what was right through countless small acts. I witnessed how her unwavering dedication to conscience shaped her life and realized that I, too, could be a force for good in the world.

Born in 1916, Dadi Janki defied the prevailing cultural norms of her time. She made incredible sacrifices for the betterment of humanity, putting aside greed and ego to act in the best interests of others. She never wavered in her pursuit of truth and fearlessness, even when it was challenging.

Her genuine love for humanity shone through in her actions, inspiring me to follow my conscience. Like Dadi Janki, you also have a conscience, and it's an invaluable tool in your arsenal. Embrace this affirmation: "Yes, I have a conscience. Yes, I will follow it. Yes, I do see myself as a good person." With this understanding, let's channel our inner conscience to achieve Soul Fitness.

I must emphasize the importance of awakening our conscience from its deep slumber. Many spiritual experiences we yearn for can be within our reach if we only pay attention to our conscience. For instance:

- Encourages self-forgiveness: A key aspect of awakening our conscience involves nurturing a sense of self-compassion and self-forgiveness.

- Enhances our potential: When we maintain a clear conscience, we can achieve much more. It serves as a powerful capacity builder.

- Fosters self-trust: By awakening our conscience, we become more trustworthy. This, in turn, helps us refrain from actions that would cause others to lose trust in us.

Alright, let's focus on awakening our conscience. How do we achieve this? By engaging in conversation, contemplation, and understanding of eternal concepts. I know I've mentioned eternal truths numerous times, but their significance cannot be overstated. It all comes down to how long we can immerse ourselves in contemplating eternal truths.

- Converse – By peacefully talking to our conscience, requesting its guidance, and asking it not to be swayed by our false ego, we can awaken it and begin to experience bliss.

- Contemplate - Contemplating eternal truth helps align our mind and intellect, bringing peace to our memory track. This tranquility then extends to our intellect and helps awaken our conscience.

- Understand - Delving deep into the understanding of eternal truths allows us to taste and experience them with our thoughts. Once we've truly tasted and experienced these eternal truths, our conscience awakens.

Awakening Your Conscience Meditation

* *Begin by focusing on your breath: Inhale deeply and exhale slowly. Allow your body to relax and your mind to become calm.*

* *Converse with your conscience: Gently direct your inner dialogue towards your conscience. Ask for its guidance and request that it remains unaffected by your false ego. Express your desire to awaken your conscience.*

* *Contemplate eternal truths: As you continue to breathe deeply, bring to mind unchanging truths that resonate with you. These could be concepts like "I am a spiritual being having a human experience" or "I am a pure, peaceful soul." Contemplate these truths and let them permeate your thoughts.*

* *Align your mind and intellect: As you contemplate these eternal truths, feel your mind and intellect aligning and coming into harmony. Envision peace spreading through your being and awakening your conscience.*

- *Awaken your conscience:* As you immerse yourself in timeless truths, feel your conscience awakening. Embrace the clarity and guidance it provides and the bliss that comes from living in alignment with your true self.

- *Return to the present:* Gently bring your awareness back to your breath. Take a few more deep breaths before returning to the present moment, feeling refreshed, grounded, and guided by your awakened conscience.

25

SOUL FITNESS ON THE GO: REAPING THE REWARDS

In this chapter, I present easy, fast, and efficient exercises for you. This is Soul Fitness on the go, that is, these practices can be performed at any time and place, even while carrying on with your everyday activities. Consistently doing these exercises, we learn how to be soul aware and regain the soul's overall health. Soul awareness entails both intellectual and experiential consciousness of the self as the soul. This awareness brings many benefits such as:

- While living and working in the world, you are aware of yourself and everyone else as a soul.
- The soul's pure qualities are active in your everyday life.
- Even in your body, you enjoy all the soul's original qualities.
- You are the master, not the slave, of your body's sense organs.

Conversely, identifying with the body ensnares us in a relentless cycle of craving, dependency, and hopelessness. When the soul is focused on seeking the utmost pleasure through physical senses, it follows the law of diminishing returns – the more we yearn for, the less satisfaction we derive. This ultimately results in profound despair. Although the consequences of body identity may be familiar, let's examine some of these outcomes:

- Lust and greed. These lead to anger because we don't get what we want when we want it.
- Arrogance. We are vain about who we are, what we did, and what we possess. This inevitably leads to emptiness since it is based on a false sense of self.
- Illusion and ignorance. When we just focus on the material world, we get trapped in the illusion of death, of a world devoid of magic and bliss.
- Body identity is the root cause of all our sorrow since it leads to insecurity, fear, ego, and attachment.

Slowly, with great care and attention, with the power of awareness, and with regular practice, we must awaken our true identity as souls. This awareness connects us to our original spiritual powers and virtues. The exercises in this chapter will help you, the soul, to remain focused on your real identity as a soul. The more you focus on being a soul, the more you will realize your full potential and experience true beauty in life.

As your original divine qualities fill your mind, purity, and innocence will overtake lust, happiness will overtake greed, love will overtake attachment, and self-respect will overtake false pride. To achieve all this, here are some simple, quick, effective exercises.

Cultivating a Balanced Relationship With the Body

In this exercise, we will experience how the soul and the body are totally connected and almost integrated. We, as human beings, are souls with a human body. That body of yours has immense value because we can't experience the physical world or our spiritual qualities without it. Hence, let's perform the following exercise while maintaining a balanced relationship between the soul and the body.

- Look at your body and with understanding talk to yourself, "This is my body. I'm the owner of this amazing arrangement of chemicals and cells."

- Now, become aware, "I, soul, am a precious point source of living light energy behind these eyes, inside this forehead."

- Next awareness, "I, soul, the spiritual being act and interact through this body. I, soul, am the source of life and life's experiences."

- Final awareness of this exercise, "I, soul, have a balanced relationship with this body."

- Keep repeating the sequence of steps from 1 to 4 till it becomes natural.

The Thinker: Discovering the Thinking, Feeling Soul

There is a need to experience who it is that is thinking. With this exercise, we will become aware of who it is that experiences feelings.

- Visualize yourself as a precious point of pulsating light energy deep inside the brain, in a place aligned with the space between, and slightly above, the eyebrows.

- You live in that wonderful physical body. That body is an amazing machine that has many physical attributes like height, weight, etc.

- You, the soul, are the thinking feeling being within that body. You can think and feel what machines cannot do, like love for your children, aspiration for a higher purpose, or elation when you see something beautiful.

- You are a precious point of conscious light energy that thinks, decides, and feels. "As the thinking, feeling being deep inside the brain, I allow the experience of pure peace to flow through me, and I express this peace through my eyes."

THE ROLE OF THE SOUL IN DRIVING THE BODY

What happens when one is driving a car and is barely aware that they are the driver of the car? Car accidents are more likely to happen. In much the same way "accidents" with the self and with others occur if we are not directing our actions from our seat in the forehead.

- You, the soul, are the driver of that car, that body. Just as the car has different elements like the engine, steering wheel, and windows, similarly, that body has sense organs. Become aware, "I, the soul, drive or use this car through the sense organs. When I get tired of using the sense organs, I become detached from the car and sleep."

- Just as the driver sees out of the front windows of the car, the eyes are the windows to your body. It is the body that has eyes, but it is the soul that sees. Pause for a moment right now from engaging the sense organs. With awareness of being light, detach from the car and rest for a moment.

- Remember, what is popularly known as death is when the driver, the soul, leaves the car, the body. If the soul, the life force, is not present in the body, the sense organs do not function. "I, soul, am the master, the driver of this "car." I drive this car with that awareness."

- Just as a car needs fuel, that body needs food to remain alive. "It is I, the soul, that eats the food, through this body. It is, I the soul, who experiences the taste of the food. This body is a machine, a car. I, the soul, show my sparkle when driving this car, this body."

Awakening the Memory of Immortality

Because the soul is not physical, nothing physical can destroy it. You, the soul, cannot be destroyed by fire, water, diseases, or bullets. This means that you always exist. You are immortal. You cannot die. Let's tap into our inherent memory of being immortal. Can you envision yourself never dying? Attempt to imagine and feel what it would be like to live eternally. This helps us recall the memory that lies dormant within us. Meditate on yourself as follows:

- "I am a luminous star, a tiny point of light. I am in my physical body but separate from it. I exist independent of it.

- "I, the soul, this point of light, being neither created nor destroyed. This is my real and true identity."

- "I have a deep conviction that I, the soul, am beyond birth and death. I will always be so. This faith comes from living and acting in my newly remembered real identity."

- "I am not created. I always exist as a tiny point of living light. I am immortal."

Path to Freedom Through the Question: Who Am I?

The right questions bring the right answers and can set us on a path to spiritual freedom. To access the wellspring of potential within, ask yourself and answer these three questions in order. Who am I? What is my form? What are my original qualities? Use visualization and understanding to answer the questions. Both understanding and visualization are important for an optimum experience. Resist going to the next question, until you've gotten something out of the preceding one.

The success of this exercise depends on how long you can stay focused on your answer, and not let other thoughts distract you. If you don't have a rewarding experience right away, just keep practicing.

Here are the answers to the three questions:

1. Who am I? "I'm a spiritual being – a soul – the immortal life force that animates this body."
2. What is my form? "I am a pulsating star - a form of living light."
3. What are my original qualities? "I am peace, and I can bring peace into my consciousness. I fully accept everything around me the way it is, I feel still and serene." (I used peace in this one, you can use other qualities the next time around.)
4. Keep repeating steps 1 through 3 again and again and again.

Viewing the Body as a Costume for the Immortal Actor Within

The soul is the life force that animates this costume we call the body. This costume has many labels. Body labels describe ethnicity, race, religion, gender, and age. All these labels distinguish our various bodily costumes. When the soul leaves the body costume (an event commonly known as death), what survives is an immortal being of light. You, the actor, never perish. Nothing can destroy you. But your costume perishes. Become aware of yourself as a soul. From that vantage point, look upon your body and mediate as follows:

- "I, the soul, the actor, use the body's eyes to look upon this bodily costume."

- "I, the soul, make this costume live. I contemplate my body and remember: I, the soul, am the life force of this costume."

- "I look at all the costume's labels -- gender, ethnicity, race, religion, and age." I remember, "I, the soul, am the actor, and this is my costume."

- "When I, the soul, leave this costume (an event commonly known as death), what survives is I, the being of immortal light. I, the actor, never perish."

- With the awareness of yourself as an actor using a bodily costume to play a part, look out through the body's eyes and watch the other actors around you play their parts.

Experiencing Being an Eternal Voyager

Let's immerse ourselves in our inherent nature of eternal existence. We are spiritual voyagers traversing through the expanse of time. Turn your thoughts inward and feel yourself as a timeless, ancient being moving through time and space with the help of a body. Keep remembering the following:

- "From the deep slumber of ignorance, I awaken to the true me. I am a soul subtle as a star. I'm real and conscious. I, the living star am beyond age, beyond time."

- "I understand myself as an eternal traveler through time. I've traveled to this material world and have become enmeshed in material things. I'm beyond time."

- "I feel myself as a timeless, ancient being moving through time and space with the help of this body. I am a traveler. This is not my permanent home."

- "In my eternal form, my light is fully ignited to its fullest capacity. I, the living star, am beautiful and wondrous."

- Eternity isn't about infinite time; it means timelessness. To truly experience eternity, let go of the past and future, focusing solely on the present moment. Once you embrace this truth, you'll find that there's nothing left to fear.

Embracing the Innate Imperishable Qualities of the Soul

The soul is conscious and intelligent; hence, the soul can absorb not only energy, but also ideas, influences, and qualities. These qualities are indestructible. Some qualities such as love, peace, purity, bliss, and knowledge are innate to the soul and also imperishable. By continuously looping the following sequence of thoughts, you can experience yourself being imperishable.

- I, the soul, am present on the seat of the body. I sit here behind these eyes as a subtle star. I cannot be seen with these physical eyes.
- I am such a tiny point of light and yet have qualities such as love, peace, and bliss within it.
- I, the soul, cannot be burnt and my qualities cannot be destroyed. This body can. I am an imperishable soul.
- I am a subtle spiritual being of light. I am imperishable.

Mastering the Soul, the Life Force of the Body

The soul occupies no space in the physical body since it is not physical, but its role is to animate and direct the body via the brain and nervous system. The soul receives messages from the body, and the body gets directions from the soul. Without the body, the soul cannot express itself and without the soul, the body doesn't function.

> - I am light. I'm pulsating and alive.
> - This pulsating light is me. Alive and aware.
> - I experience that I am the life force in this body. The conscient light energy that animates this body.
> - I've adopted this body to experience the physical world but I'm not the body. I'm a spiritual being – a soul – the life force that animates this body.

THE SACRED TEMPLE: REVERING THE BODY

This body is not merely a costume. It is also a temple. It is sacred and we need to revere it and not defile it. Therein lies its greatest value. Recognize this value and take good care of the bodily temple. While in this body, we can all transform our consciousness.

> - I am a soul, and this body is my temple.
> - I, the soul, see my body through its own eyes, and I vow to treat it as a golden temple.
> - I am divine light in this temple. This is my true identity. I am pure spirit, a form of living divine light.

> - As I take each step, I remind myself that I am a pure, divine spirit residing within my physical body. When I, as the soul, recognize and embrace my soul identity, this awareness has a multitude of positive effects on my body. It can improve my overall well-being, reduce stress, and even heal and maintain balance.

BEYOND GENDER: EMBRACING SOUL AWARENESS FOR SPIRITUAL TRANSFORMATION

This exercise helps us honor and nurture the body as a vehicle for spiritual transformation. It requires making a conscious choice to connect with your original self and recreating your self-image based on your original intrinsic divine qualities. Your gender is not the actual you, your spiritual identity. Each gender identity has its set patterns of thinking and acting and most importantly limitations. In contrast, when you are soul conscious and consciously aware of your existence as a soul, you awaken to a world of possibility. A world where there is no weight of centuries of baggage associated with gender. This aspect of soul consciousness is the seed of happiness.

> - The thinking feeling being is I, the soul. I live here in this forehead, behind these eyes, right behind the center of my eyebrows. I am light.
>
> - I recognize the limitations that the identification of my gender can put on my feelings.

- Gently but firmly, I shift my thoughts to understand myself as a spiritual being. I see myself as a point of divine light.
- I choose to see each person beyond their gender – each person as a sparkling point of light behind the eyes.

SOUL AND BODY: A PARTNERSHIP OF ELECTRICITY AND LIGHT BULB

We all know electric light is the most common form of artificial lighting and is essential to modern society. And both electricity and the light bulb need to be combined to provide light. Similarly, the soul, the source of life, enlivens the body. Just as electrical energy is transformed, in the light bulb, into heat and light, similarly, soul energy is transformed in the body into living, breathing, and experiencing being.

- Visualize a dark room. In this room, see a point of light sparkling bright in front of you. Switch on your awareness and realize that this being of light is you, the soul.
- Now, visualize this sparkling bright light animating your body. Remember, "This is my body, the light bulb. I'm the electricity of this body."

- Deeply with understanding, "I realize that just as electricity and a light bulb need to be combined to function, I, the soul, and this body act in partnership to experience and express a human existence."
- "I am pure spirit, a form of living light energy."

The Puppeteer Within

Just as a puppeteer manipulates a puppet to create the illusion that the puppet is "alive," the soul, the puppeteer, manipulates the puppet, the body. Loop the following sequence of thoughts in your mind for a beautiful experience:

- I am a sparkling, pure light housed within the body. This body is just a puppet of the five elements.
- I, the puppeteer, make this puppet perform.
- I, the soul, animate it and bring peaceful expression to it. I, the soul, the puppeteer is hidden from the audience.
- I choose to express peace through this puppet of the five elements.

The Guest Within

When we are guests in someone's house, we behave very differently than when we think it is our own home. For example, if we are good guests, we respect our host's belongings, and we won't use anything we haven't been permitted to use. We pick up after ourselves and have minimum expectations. When we know something doesn't belong to us or if we know we are going to be somewhere temporarily, then we won't get bent out of shape if things are not exactly the way we want them to be.

When we are aware of being a guest in this body, we experience deep contentment. Also, when you consider yourself to be a guest, you become free from attachment to how your body looks. This exercise brings out the best guest qualities in us.

- I, the soul, am shining and seated in between my eyebrows behind these eyes.
- I'm here in this body temporarily. I am a guest in this body. This human form is temporary and will age and fall away as all material things do.
- Nothing belongs to me, the guest. As a guest, I'm given this body to use for my needs, but there is no feeling of it belonging to me. I am detached yet loving while using this body with great care.
- This body is not I; I'm just a guest traveling through time seated in this temporary body. I keep reminding myself again and again – I am the soul within, a guest in this body.

From Seed to Sprout: Awakening Hidden Potential

This awareness of the seed form makes you, the soul, full of all experiences. It helps you keep the past in the past and be full in just being the seed. Loop the following thoughts in your mind:

- Visualize a small seed planted in the ground. It is slowly sprouting. Two leaves emerge from this seed. Watch It slowly become a small sapling. As you watch this seed sprout, you realize everything is within that seed. The DNA of a whole big tree and all the fruit is contained within the seed.

- Now, become aware of yourself as a pulsating subtle seed of light. Spiritual powers, wisdom, understanding, and virtues are latent within you, the soul, the seed. When you, the soul, enter that body, your qualities emerge as you play your part.

- Now, gently but firmly leave the outside things outside and focus on just being the spiritual seed.

- Remember: Your original qualities are contained within you, the soul. Keep repeating to yourself with understanding, "I, the soul, am a seed."

Opening the Third Eye

With your third eye open, you can see beyond the physical into the true nature of reality. With this exercise, you, the soul, will become a powerful master and go beyond the limitations of the material world. You will feel prosperous! Loop the following sequence of thoughts in your mind:

- I, the soul, am a tiny dot. I'm eternal, unique, and unhindered by time and space. I'm pure spiritual light energy.
- I'm located here, behind these eyes at the base of the brain, the engine of the body. This is where the third eye of wisdom has been shown.
- It is I, the soul, that seeks wisdom and divine sight. I open my third eye and awaken to my true consciousness.
- I realize that I stumbled around in darkness and ignorance before my third eye was open. When I open my third eye, there is light, and the darkness is dispelled. I recognize me, know me, and love me.

Timer Meditation: A Technique for Enhancing Focus

This is a powerful exercise designed to improve your concentration and deepen your connection to your true self. In this exercise, we explore the transformative technique of using a timer to cultivate focus and self-awareness in just a few minutes a day.

To perform a timer meditation using your phone, follow these steps:

- Open the clock app on your phone and set a timer for your desired meditation duration, such as one, two, or three minutes. Begin with a one-minute session and gradually increase the duration as you become more comfortable with the practice.

- During the meditation, focus on either the concept of being a soul or on a specific primary quality of the soul, like love, peace, bliss, purity, or wisdom.

- While meditating, be aware of two things:

- Keep track of how many times your mind wanders from the focus. Use your fingers to count each time it does so. For example, if you are concentrating on being a soul and your mind drifts to an unrelated thought, count it on your fingers.

- When your mind wanders, make a conscious effort to bring it back to the meditation focus.

This technique may be advanced for beginners, but it is effective in improving concentration and experiencing the soul. The key is to notice when your mind wanders and consciously bring it back to the practice. Over time, you'll find that this timer meditation helps you develop better focus and a deeper understanding of your inner self, regardless of how often your mind wanders during the meditation.

**Access free meditations to go deeper
into your quest for immortality**

These Soul Fitness meditations will pave the way for your true spiritual nature to unfold, illuminate, and spread joy to yourself and the world.

Go here to get access now:

shireenchada.com/soulfitness

26

COMMAND YOUR SENSES, MASTER YOURSELF

The image that comes to mind when I think of the connection between body, soul, and senses is a horse-drawn carriage. Visualize five horses pulling a carriage along a cobbled street at a brisk trot. Now what would happen if one of the horses gets distracted? Or if the driver gets distracted or forgets he is driving the carriage? In this analogy, you, the soul, are the driver of the carriage. The carriage is the body, and the horses are the body's five senses.

As a skilled driver expertly handles the reins, you, the soul, should maintain control over your senses. Utilize your senses while remaining in command, ensuring a safe journey. When a driver loses control over their horses, danger follows. Similarly, when influenced by sensory indulgences, possessions, and attachments, the soul can lose control of the body. This loss of control stems from forgetting our true nature as eternal, conscious souls residing within the vessel of the body.

Lack of knowledge and not accepting the self as a soul is the cause of our feelings of emptiness and dissatisfaction. The soul then tries to fill this void by gratifying the body's desires. The happiness of sense gratification is only temporary and obeys the law of diminishing returns, first described by economists. They explained that beyond a certain point, additional inputs produce smaller and smaller outputs. The same occurs when we seek happiness through the senses. At a certain point, further attempts at happiness yield diminishing returns. The much-coveted gratification fades over time, leading to dependency, addiction, and self-destructive behavior.

We are all trapped by our senses; hence we must control and master them. In this chapter, I provide simple, effective exercises that make you the master, the driver, of your physical senses.

Overcoming Illusion and Gaining Control Over Our Eyes

For millennia, sages have argued that the eyes and ears take priority over the other sense organs. Think about it -- almost from birth, we take delight in visible objects, thinking they will give us happiness. We assume that visual pleasures are the path to happiness. This may be most misleading since the lust to see certain objects can be the root of all *f,* or illusion. For millennia, the wise have warned us about this dangerous illusion. So, let's heed their advice and do a simple exercise to gain control over our eyes.

- Find a quiet spot and sit comfortably. Pick an object close to you and take a good look at it. If you are outside, this could be a tree; if you are inside, this could be a bookcase, lamp, or any fixed object.

- Now, slowly begin to focus your eyes on the tip of your nose. From your nose, pull your consciousness inside, into the center of your forehead. Become aware of yourself as a soul.

- Now, shift your attention to the soul. Silently say to yourself, "I, the soul, am the one seeing that object through these eyes."

- Now, go back to looking at the object. Then, again, slowly bring your attention back to yourself as a soul. Go back and forth between being aware of yourself as a soul and looking at the object. Do this at least five or six times.

- Keep reminding yourself that "I, the soul, will decide where my eyes focus and what I, the soul, will see." When you rise and move around, have a silent conversation with yourself, "I can choose to use my eyes only to see things that will bring me lasting benefit."

Tuning The Ears: Overcoming Emotional Turmoil

The Bhagavad Gita (5.22) says, "Indeed those pleasures born of sense-contact are merely sources of pain." This especially seems to be true with our ears. Take the case of lovers. We want to hear sweet nothings from our lover and a few years down the line, with the same ears, we hear harsh things from the same person, and we begin to feel extreme pain. Let's do the following exercise to stop this vicious cycle:

- Sit in a comfortable position where you can be still for a few moments. Take a deep breath, release that breath, and pause for a moment. Now hear the ambient sounds around you. It could be the birds chirping, the noise of the air conditioner, or traffic noise.

- Now, gently pull your awareness from the external world to your inner being. Become aware of yourself as the soul, the light energy that animates that body.

- Remind yourself, "I, the soul, am the one who is using these ears of the body to hear these sounds."

- Now, hear the ambient sounds again. Then again, slowly bring your attention back to your eternal self. Keep doing this a few times.

- While going about your daily life, have a silent conversation with yourself, "I, the soul, am the master; I can choose what I listen to and take in and what I let pass. I can choose to just take in those words that elevate the soul and bring wisdom and joy to the self."

Practicing Detachment from Sense of Smell

This exercise can be used when we smell something, and it triggers memories or unhealthy habits. Like in the previous two exercises, in this one too, we will engage the concept of the senses not being the eternal self. Like the turtle that retracts from its limbs, let's practice going inwards and detaching from our sense of smell.

- Take a deep breath, release that breath, and smell your surroundings. Take another deep breath and release that breath. Now, let's do it once more. While breathing deeply, you will automatically become aware of the ambient smells.

- Now become aware of yourself as the soul, the light energy that animates that body. Slowly, bring your attention to the ambient smells again.

- Go back and forth between being a soul, and using your nose to smell. Remind yourself, "I, the soul, am the one who uses this nose to smell."

- Silently talk to yourself, "I, the soul, am the one smelling through this nose. I can choose to keep my peace even when I'm smelling a bad odor."

Overcome Emotional Eating to Cultivate Balance

As I mentioned in the ears exercise, the Bhagavad Gita (5.22) describes the senses as sources of suffering. It goes on to say, "Such pleasures possess a beginning and an end." This is never more true than with our sense of taste. Try the following exercise as an experiment to control emotional eating.

- Do this exercise before meals and snacks. Before you put food in your mouth, move your tongue around your mouth and taste your saliva.

- Now, gently but firmly pull your attention to your eternal self. That is, become aware of yourself as a soul, divine light.

- Now, take a bite while being aware of yourself as an eternal soul. Focus on the taste in your mouth and gently but firmly see yourself as the soul, tasting through the mouth.

- Go back and forth between the taste in your mouth and awareness of yourself as a soul.

- Every time you take a bite, keep repeating silently to yourself, "I, the soul, am the master of my taste. I decide what I eat and don't eat, what I taste and don't taste."

MASTERING THE SENSE OF TOUCH

With this exercise, you can free yourself from being a slave to touch or feel. This includes temperature comfort of cool or hot. It also includes how the sun, rain, or the texture of the clothes feel against your skin. When we rely too heavily on any of these sensations or if our mood is based on them to make us feel happy then we are setting ourselves up for taking sorrow from them. The following is a simple exercise to gain control over our sense of touch.

- Sit in a quiet spot and breathe in and out deeply. Meditate on your breath for a few moments. Pick up a small object close to you and feel it around in your hands. This should be something other than your phone or any other electronic object. Pick up something natural, like a small stone. Feel the object in your hand. Notice how your sense of touch is attuned to the object.

- While still holding the object, gently but firmly, become aware of yourself as a soul, luminous light energy.

- Now, shift your attention to the object again and feel it in your hands. Again, shift your attention to your eternal self. Go back and forth by shifting your attention to the object and then shifting it back to your eternal luminous self.

- Silently have a conversation with the self, "I, the soul, am the one touching and feeling this object."

Mastering the Art of Speech

How many times did you get into trouble because you put your foot in your mouth? Do you want to improve the way you say things? This exercise might help you. Though speaking is traditionally not a sense organ, I thought to include it here because it is so key to gaining command over what we say.

- Sit comfortably and alone in a quiet room. Now, recall, something you've said during the last week or month that you could have said better. Say it aloud again now that you are alone.

- Bring your attention to yourself as a soul, the luminous light that animates this body.

- Remind yourself, "I, the soul, am the one who used the sense of speech to say these words."

- Now think of a better way to say it and say it aloud.

- Go within again, and remember the eternal self. Bring your awareness to the external body and meditate on yourself speaking through the mouth.

- Repeatedly say to yourself, "I, the soul, the master, choose to think before I speak, and let only jewels of goodness emerge from these lips. I choose to use my words to bring sweetness and joy into the world today."

27
STRESS BUSTER MEDITATIONS

The placement of these meditations at the end of the book is intentional. As the saying goes, it's better to teach someone to fish rather than simply providing them with fish. The exercises in chapters x, y, and z are crafted to help you tackle stress, anxiety, and depression holistically. The examples below demonstrate how you can combine and adapt the exercises to create custom meditations tailored to your needs.

DEALING WITH DEPRESSION

This meditation is designed for people who suffer from low-grade depression, such as persistent low mood, loss of motivation, hopelessness, or low self-esteem. If you are clinically depressed, then consult with a doctor in addition to doing this meditation.

Along with this meditation, I invite you to change some personal habits. To begin with: 1. Start exercising daily. 2. Get off alcohol, processed sugar, and recreational drugs. 3. Pick up a hobby that doesn't involve smartphones, computers, or a TV.

The first step in dealing with depression is to be aware of the chatter in our heads. Just observe the voice in your head. If it is easier for you to observe if you write, then write down the obsessive thoughts going on in your head. Now, gently but firmly tell yourself, "I have a choice. I can transform these thoughts into powerful thoughts filled with vitality." There is an intimate connection between our thoughts and depression.

The second step in dealing with depression is to think of your depression as an invitation to go deeper into your soul. Respond to it rather than wishing it will just go away. Open your mind and tell yourself, "Yes, I am ready; I will go deeper into my soul. I want to live in a much more beautiful internal space." Our internal space is dependent on our awareness. If we change our awareness, we transform our inner space.

The third step in dealing with depression is to have patience. Think of your depression as the winter of your mental rhythm. Just like at the end of winter, how bulbs begin to slowly take shape, how flowers start to form, and seeds begin the process of germination, in much the same way, when you are depressed, you have to have faith that if you do a daily practice of meditation and spend time in your soul, then the work of that spiritual effort will be revealed. You will wake up one day, and you will realize that the spring of your mental rhythm has arrived, and you will feel so much better. Keep this in mind before you give up.

So are you ready? Let's meditate.

* *Imagine now that you are traveling in your mind far, far away from this world of dramas. You sense yourself getting quieter and quieter as the world of stories disappears. Take a deep breath. As you exhale, the world of sound vanishes, and you are in this present moment, in silent communion with yourself. You bask in the feeling of being a luminous, quiet being. Let this beautiful world of silence wash over you like a soft breeze as you absorb the gentle, comforting energy of serenity. Allow yourself to let go and simply receive whatever this moment has to offer. Take your time and absorb this energy. Now you feel ready for the next step on your inner journey.*

* *In this state of relaxation, you are connected to your core being, to the real you . . . You are an eternal soul . . . Now, take a few moments and give thanks for three things in your life. Feel grateful for simple and big things in your life . . . This feeling of gratitude calms and restores you.*

* *Now, you are ready to go into the soul and contemplate: Who am I really? You contemplate this concept that Shakespeare first proposed, "All the world's a stage. And all the men and women merely players; they have their exits and their entrances, and one man in his time plays many parts . . ." You accept, "Yes, this is a play. I, the soul, am an actor. In this life, the events that have occurred to me are part of the whole cosmic play. What happened externally doesn't define me. I, the soul, don't identify with them."*

* *"I, the soul, am a beautiful being of energy, of love, of light. At the core, I am a divine being, an absolutely beautiful spirit."*

* *"I can't necessarily control the external scenes of this cosmic play, but, as an actor of this play, I choose to live in joy." "I came as a beautiful being into this cosmic play, and I'm just passing through. I have the choice to express my beautiful qualities through my story."*

* *Don't take anything that happens in the play personally. Talk to yourself, "Nothing that happened externally in the past means anything about who I am internally."*

* *With determination tell yourself, "For a few moments each day, I choose to live in the present moment, practice having an attitude of gratitude, and I'm not going to make my present life about my past dramas." Stop believing the negative stories you are telling yourself.*

* *Dealing with depression with a daily dose of wisdom is like going from winter to spring. Spring is definitely on the way. Your process of healing has begun.*

* *Slowly come back to your real self, here and now, feeling refreshed, wise, and strong. Now stay in Soul Fitness and shine your light on the world.*

DEALING WITH INSOMNIA

To conquer insomnia, we need a quiet, comfortable sleep environment and a relaxing bedtime routine – doctors call this sleep hygiene. To achieve this, make sure that:

1. Your bedroom is dark, quiet, and comfortably cool.
2. You turn off all screens such as TV, computer, and cell phone at least one hour before bedtime.
3. You put all your electronic devices in another room.
4. You don't drink anything at least one hour before bedtime.
5. You keep a worry-delay journal in which you write down your worries and tell yourself that you will think about them tomorrow.

Many times we get so stressed from not being able to sleep that that stress itself will not allow us to sleep. So make relaxation your goal not sleep. Unlike drugs, which are often effective at first, but lose their power over time, the following relaxation exercise gains in power with repetition and practice.

So, are you ready? Let's meditate.

* *You are resting on your bed. Allow yourself to drift away from the world of sounds and sights and travel within to a deep place of relaxation. Feel the mattress below you.*

* *Now imagine that all your tensions are pouring into the mattress below you. At this moment, release your thoughts - whatever you don't need. And, let the mattress absorbs them. You are relaxed.*

* *Alright, let's try a breathing technique by Andrew Weil that does wonders for me. Start by exhaling fully through your mouth, creating a whoosh sound. Close your mouth and take a quiet breath through your nose, counting to four in your head. Hold that breath for a seven-count.*

Then, release the air from your mouth with a whoosh sound, counting to eight. That's one full breath.

* *Let's do this breathing technique three more times. Exhale all the air from your mouth with a whoosh sound. Keep your mouth closed and breathe in through your nose, mentally counting to four. Hold your breath for seven counts. After that, exhale through your mouth with a whoosh sound, counting to eight. You've just completed your second breath.*

* *Let's do this breathing technique two more times. Again, exhale fully through your mouth with a whoosh sound. Inhale through your nose with your mouth closed, counting to four in your head. Hold your breath for seven counts. Then, exhale with a whoosh sound through your mouth, counting to eight. That's your third breath.*

* *Now, let's do this breathing technique one last time— Exhale completely with a whoosh sound through your mouth. Close your mouth, and inhale quietly through your nose, mentally counting to four. Hold your breath for a count of seven. Finally, exhale with a whoosh sound through your mouth, counting to eight. You've completed the fourth and final breath.*

* *This breathing technique helps you to sink deeply into a peaceful, calm, and serene state. You are now completely relaxed.*

* *Now, let's get your body even more relaxed. Close your eyes, focus your mind on your feet, fill them up with light, then tense them up, and then let them go – surrender them to gravity. Your feet should feel heavy now, and then visualize this light coming up from your feet to your*

ankles. Focus on your ankles now, fill them with light, tense them, and then let go - - surrender them to gravity. Your feet and ankles are relaxed and heavy now.

* *Now, let the light travel up to your lower legs.*
* *Fill them with light, tense them, and then let them go - - surrender them to gravity. Your lower legs are totally relaxed and heavy now.*
* *Now let the light travel up to your thighs.*
* *Fill them with light, tense them, and then let them go - - surrender them to gravity. Your thighs are totally relaxed and heavy now.*
* *Now let the light travel up to your hips.*
* *Fill them with light, tense them, and then let them go - - surrender them to gravity. Your hips are totally relaxed and heavy now.*
* *Now let the light travel up to your stomach.*
* *Fill it with light, tense it, and then let it go - - surrender it to gravity. Your stomach is totally relaxed and heavy now.*
* *Now let the light travel up to your chest.*
* *Fill it with light, tense it, and then let it go - - surrender it to gravity. Your chest is totally relaxed and heavy now.*
* *Now let the light travel up to your shoulder.*
* *Fill it up with light, tense it up, and then let it go - - surrender it to gravity. Your shoulder is totally relaxed and heavy now.*

* *Now let the light travel up to your arms.*
* *Fill them up with light, tense them up, and then let them go -- surrender them to gravity. Your arms are totally relaxed and heavy now.*
* *Now let the light travel up to your neck.*
* *Fill it up with light, tense it up, and then let it go -- surrender it to gravity. Your neck is totally relaxed and heavy now.*
* *Now let the light travel up to your face and head.*
* *Fill them up with light, tense them up, and then let them go -- surrender them to gravity. Your face and head are totally relaxed now.*
* *Now focus all the light in the center of your forehead. At this moment, all you feel is total tranquility. Remain aware of yourself as light and silently say to yourself, "I am totally relaxed. I am totally relaxed."*
* *Slowly you feel relaxed and restful and sleepy.*

I've incorporated a warm-up exercise for the above meditation. Many of the warm-up exercises can be combined with the mind aerobic exercises to come up with dynamic stress-buster routines.

BUILD BETTER RELATIONSHIPS

* *Take a deep breath and while releasing this breath, move into your center. Take another deep breath and release this breath while going deeper into your center. Continue to breathe deeply in and out . . . in and out . . . as you connect with your still core. Rest for a few moments in your serene, silent center. Now visualize a waterfall of pure, clean, light pouring onto you. This light feels like refreshing waters that cleanse away all that you no longer need. As this light flows over you, it's as if the old you are washed away and all that is left is a fresh, clean, new you.*

* *In this refreshed state, you are ready to build better relationships. The first step is not to suppress the self. Rather affirm to yourself again and again, "I will learn to communicate better. There is a solution to every problem. I will find mutual understanding." You take care to have only positive conversations within your head. You begin to develop faith and trust in yourself and others.*

* *The second step to building good relationships is to remain neutral in your feelings. Tell yourself, "I'm a well-wisher of everyone. I will not take sides. No one is all good, nor is there anyone who is all bad." You step away from like and dislike and have a vision of compassion and cooperation toward everyone. Remember that to keep someone's mistakes in your awareness is like ingesting poison. Deep down, every soul is truth and love. Tell yourself, "I will learn to focus on that, and in doing so, help them to reveal it." "I will not give up hope on anyone."*

* *The third step in building good relationships is going deeply into pure, powerful thoughts. You have pure thoughts such as, "I am spirit. I am complete with peace, love, and wisdom. These qualities exist within me forever, and I lost touch with them only because I forgot who I am. I am light, I am eternal, and I am love."*

* *Through such pure, compelling thoughts, your words, actions, and most importantly your relationships begin to heal . . . You understand that your thoughts determine your response to the people around you. You keep the faith and trust in yourself and maintain powerful thoughts. This trust brings contentment to your relationships.*

COMBAT THE STRESS OF CONSUMERISM

Dear readers, nowadays, we are all surrounded by people who seek satisfaction in acquiring more material things. We may be one of them. The goal of this meditation is to help you to feel better about yourself in such a world and to free yourself from the compulsive accumulation and consumption of material goods that may only create more anxiety in your life. You probably already know that excessive consumption is an emotional deficit, not an asset. This desire to keep up with the Joneses drags us down in the long run. We can transcend this attachment to material things and the anxiety it causes by realizing the truth of who we really are. To fully benefit from this meditation, read it a few times.

Let's be quiet for a few moments and reflect on our relationship with ourselves. For too many of us, material things form the basis of our self-worth. We place too much attention on what we own. Consumerism cages most of us. We often get trapped by comparing ourselves to others, forgetting how silly it is to think, "The golden bars of my neighbor's cage are better than the iron bars of mine." A cage is a cage is a cage! Mentally and spiritually, we seem to be shackled.

At this moment, you have the power to step outside the consumer cage. Outside of this cage, you are a sacred being. A spiritual being. You are eternal - you always exist. You are gifted. You are light. Your life is sacred.

It is time to enter into a new paradigm and the new way of thinking it inspires. Sit quietly and ask yourself, "What is the single most important change in thinking that will help me move toward greater freedom and security?

Take a moment now and think about these questions. On deep reflection, you realize that the single most important change in thinking that will help you move toward greater freedom and security is to cultivate new thought patterns.

* *Sit quietly and say to yourself, "To cultivate new thought patterns I need solitude. Spiritual solitude is absolutely essential for me right now."*

* *Visualize yourself sitting at dawn on the shore of a still lake. As you keep watching the lake, you begin to absorb its stillness. At this moment, you are only aware of the serenity and beauty of this lake. Even though it is tempting to think of your problems, give your mind a much-needed rest and fix it on the tranquility of the scene before*

you. Keep looking at the lake and keep absorbing its stillness till you feel a profound silence within.

* *In this silence, you trust. From this place of trust, you let go, you let go of your cage, you let go of your limited self, you allow yourself to let go of your attachment . . . You trust in simplicity bringing you greater joy, and you fly, you fly to be with your real, authentic, eternal spiritual self.*

* *You fly up past the sky, beyond the stars, and you keep flying till you reach a universe of golden orange light. Don't stop there. Keep flying till you reach the pinnacle of this pulsating universe of light. There, at the apex is a beautiful, luminous light. You touch this light, and as soon as you feel the light, you start radiating the intrinsically good qualities of your soul. This light illumines the darkness of your mind and makes you free. You are flying freely. Here in this realm, you feel totally secure. You experience your real self, and you touch your eternity.*

* *From this place of strength and freedom, you give generously. You give your gifts to the world. You give for as many moments as possible. You give your peace, and you give your joy. You give abundantly and to as many people as possible. Because you understand, my friend, that only in giving is there receiving. Only in giving do you feel the joy of your treasure.*

* *Remember you are eternal, remember your life is sacred, remember you have unique gifts, and remember that ultimately only in giving do you receive - This is your true value, your real worth. Remind yourself of this again and again and again.*

Deal With Work Stress

Work might sometimes feel like being in a pressure cooker. Too much work, interpersonal conflicts, unfulfilled career goals, being left out of decision-making, and multiple other stresses at work might make you feel like you are stewed, fried, and grilled at the same time. If the heat is getting to you, this meditation is for you.

* *Slowly breathe in and out as you move into your center. With each breath, allow yourself to go deeper and deeper into that quiet center within. Imagine that deep inside you there is a switch that can turn off the heat. Slowly and deliberately turn this switch off now. The chatter and noise in your mind slowly disappear, and you can relax into profound stillness.*

* *Breathe in the moment and rest in this stillness for that moment. You now understand that this stress and pressure are trying to tell you something.*

* *Take another deep breath. As you exhale, you feel quieter. Rest in this peaceful space for a few moments and ask yourself, "What is the message that this stress is bringing?" "What is the gift?" The difficulty here is that we try to control things that are not in our control, or we live in the past or worry about the future, and so we imprison ourselves.*

* *Say to yourself, "I deeply accept that my stress at work has come as a change agent. It is telling me I need to make some minor or major changes in the way I think and my outlook on life." Just remember again and again that you can and will manage what is happening externally.*

Reframe your work stress as a signal to the self, to your inner being to become more resilient . . .

* *Stress is merely a sign of the times, and it reveals that you are seeking support in the wrong places. Life moves in cycles; it is continually changing - We have the power in life to build or to break down. You have the power at this moment to create a new positive pattern. This skill to manage your stress is within you; you simply must remember your true eternal identity, for the skill and the power are within your true self*

* *Now, enter into pure awareness of being an eternal soul. In this state of consciousness, you are beyond any of your labels such as gender or race or even things like, "I am intelligent or skillful." Keep remembering, "I am a spiritual being. This human body that I occupy is not me." "I am not the labels assigned to this body." Now, gently but firmly step outside the identity defined by what you do and enter into the pure expanse of your eternal being. You are so much more than what you do for a living. Say to yourself again and again, "I am eternal. My original nature is peace, wisdom, and joy. I am divine at the core of my true self."*

* *Commit yourself, "I will regularly take time to reframe my work stress." This helps you to reawaken your self-worth and transforms your work. You see the situations at your job as a game, a game that you can win just by changing your attitude. You begin to feel a renewed sense of calmness, confidence, and clarity. You feel whole and restored by this awareness.*

28

CHOOSING SOUL FITNESS

Our modern society often values material possessions and external success over the quality of our inner lives. This focus on materialism can create a lot of pressure and burden on individuals, leading to a disconnection from the deeper aspects of life, such as quality, care, and sensitivity.

Research has shown that people with a healthy mind, a strong will, and a positive attitude recover quicker from illness and accidents. How come we can't seem to manage these seemingly simple abilities? It all boils down to the psychological limitations we impose upon ourselves -- a false limiting identity of being just a physical body and its labels. We are the ones who imprison ourselves in this illusion and we are the only ones who can free ourselves.

You have within you both the sources of any suffering as well as the solution to it. Ultimately each of us elevates or degrades ourselves: self alone is the self's friend or enemy; it is our choice.

[Bagwad Gita 6.5–6]

Hence, it is advisable to thoroughly contemplate the contents of this book before taking any action, as we are blessed with free will, but the repercussions of our choices cannot be escaped. Always keep in mind:

- Change implies responsibility for the state of your mind and your actions. Becoming a master of your thoughts, feelings, reactions, and responses means you cut puppet consciousness—being pulled here and there by everything and everyone, getting into cycles of bad feelings, blaming, complaining, and accusing.
- The intellect has a crucial role in guiding and transforming the self. The positive qualities, which are in you as *sanskars* can only be brought to the surface of the conscious mind through the intervention of the intellect, which is totally dependent on you.

Make the most important choice of your life wisely, dear readers. Trust your inner voice and intuition, and opt for the path of Soul Fitness because:

- Soul Fitness provides a sense of grounding, peace, and clarity amidst the daily chaos, allowing you to navigate through life's challenges with greater ease and stability.
- Incorporating Soul Fitness into your daily life can help you access the spiritual world, allowing you to gain a deeper understanding of the interconnectedness of all things and tap into a wellspring of wisdom and guidance that transcends your limitations.

- Engaging in Soul Fitness isn't about striving for perfection or a specific outcome but rather about embracing your spiritual nature and being fully present in each moment. By doing so, you can infuse your life with a sense of renewed wonder and joy.
- Practicing Soul Fitness can elevate your consciousness and bring you a greater sense of fulfillment, purpose, and connection to the world around you. Take that first step and embark on a transformative spiritual journey that can enrich your life in countless ways.

Access free meditations to go deeper into your quest for immortality:

These Soul Fitness meditations will pave the way for your true spiritual nature to unfold, illuminate, and spread joy to yourself and the world.

Go here to get access now:

shireenchada.com/soulfitness

ACKNOWLEDGMENTS

As I begin to express sincere thanks to those who so kindly helped me with this book, an old saying comes to mind: It takes a village to raise a child. This, I discovered, is equally true in the writing of this book - the fruit of seven years of labor and the active support of a caring village. Perhaps I can offer a variation on the old saying: "A community, with love, guides a book into existence, combined with seven years of diligent authorial effort." This process has resulted in a book that I am confident will prove to be a valuable resource in your journey through life.

A small group of close friends and family rendered extraordinary help. You know who you are, and how grateful I am.

Every soul within my circle of life has contributed to this venture through their love, combined wisdom, and ceaseless enthusiasm. I extend my sincere gratitude to all of them.